Praise for **THE FOUR VOICES**

Pat Morley is an amazing writer and an even better person. His books aren't just written—they are lived. There is an old adage: the battle is won or lost in the mind. If that's true, and I believe it is, this book is a game changer! Who is the loudest voice in your life? This book will help you turn down the volume on the wrong voices, and turn up the volume on the still small voice of the Holy Spirit.

Mark Batterson

New York Times best-selling author of *The Circle Maker*
Lead Pastor of National Community Church

If you've struggled to get a handle on what's going on in your thought life, here's your opportunity! Great book at just the right time! Read it and let it soak your mind with God's plan for taking charge of your heart and head. Very readable and biblical, with compelling stories and illustrations. You're going to love this book!

Gary Chapman, Ph.D.

Author of *The 5 Love Languages*

Such an important and timely book! What a relief to know that not everything that goes through my head is just "me"!

John Eldredge

Author of *Wild at Heart*

Patrick Morley has done it again! The Four Voices will equip you to make sense of the voices in your head. Best of all, it's totally based on Scripture. Read it. Absorb it. Let it renew your mind. This book will help you get on top of the thoughts that have been trying to get on top of you!

Dr. Tony Evans
President, The Urban Alternative
Senior Pastor, Oak Cliff Bible Fellowship

In my opinion, this is Pat's best book. It's wise, it's practical and it's thoroughly biblical.

Steve Farrar
Chairman, Men's Leadership Ministries

The competing dialogue in our head isn't just last night's pizza. Pat teaches us how to discern the Holy Spirit's voice from the three most destructive voices that threaten our joy and peace and keep us from the will of God in our lives.

Dave Ramsey
Best-Selling Author and Radio Host

For many years I've been challenged by "voices" I hear in my head. The assignment for us is to speak unvarnished truth right back to them. As he does so well, my friend Patrick nails this and helps us navigate the potential treachery that could be in store if we let these voices sneak up on us.

Robert Wolgemuth
Best-Selling Author

THE
FOUR
VOICES

TAKING CONTROL OF
THE CONVERSATION
IN YOUR HEAD

PATRICK MORLEY

MIM Press

The Four Voices
Copyright © 2021 by Patrick Morley

Requests for information should be addressed to:
Man in the Mirror, *1375 State Road 436, Casselberry, Florida
32707*

ISBN 978-0-578-88140-9

Cover design: Jeremy Kennedy
Layout and interior design: Carolyn Bennett Fraiser

MIM Press is an imprint of Man in the Mirror, Inc.

Printed in the United States of America

DEDICATION

To the men
who showed me the way:

Jim Gillean

Lyle Nelsen

Dan Stanley

CONTENTS

Introduction

Are you tired of feeling confused or overwhelmed by the voices competing for control of your head and heart? If so, you're not alone. These voices can be helpful, frustrating, discouraging, or even dangerous.

In *The Four Voices*, you're going to learn what those voices are, where they come from, and how you can take control of the conversation. We all go to dark places from time to time, but we don't have to stay there. You can do a lot to help yourself, and I'm going to show you how.

The Four Voices is based on the belief that we should read the Bible to understand our experiences. That said, you don't have to be a Christian to understand what's been written.

But if you're not, I hope you will find enough here to become a man or woman of faith or, at a minimum, better understand the Christian view of what's influencing your thoughts, words, and actions.

I'm trained in theology and business, not psychology or counseling, so I've made no attempt to synthesize what I know about Scripture with the behavioral sciences. I will leave that to trained professionals, many of whose contributions to mental health and human well-being are quite remarkable—especially those of faith-based practitioners. If after reading this book you still feel like you have unresolved thoughts and feelings, then I strongly encourage you to seek professional help.

Let's begin with an overview of what's going on inside.

ONE

What's Going On Inside Your Head?

*Above all else, guard your heart,
for everything you do flows from it.*

Proverbs 4:23

One warm Florida day near the end of fourth grade, I walked into a convenience store and saw a freezer display packed full of ice cream sandwiches. At that moment, I wanted an ice cream sandwich as much as I've ever wanted anything, but I didn't have enough money.

Then a voice whispered, "It's okay. Go ahead and take one. No one will ever know." So, I tucked one under my shirt and walked out the door.

Immediately another voice started telling me, "You were not raised like this. You need to take it back."

Suddenly, I felt like the rope in a titanic tug of war. I had a choice to make. (I did take it back). However, as adults, we all know the tug of war only intensifies as the stakes go up, as illustrated in these three situations.

———

Situation #1: Brad has built a highly respected and successful property and casualty insurance business. In a courageously transparent

"I don't feel like people care about me, only what I can do for them."

moment, he told eight of us in a small group, "I don't feel like people care about me—only what I can do for them."

I was flabbergasted. Brad and I have been involved in ministry together since his college days. I love him to death. He's one of the finest men I've ever known. I know firsthand how much his wife and three children adore him. As his client, I've seen how much his employees admire and respect him. Many of his other clients are also friends of mine, and they openly express their appreciation and affection for him.

Why would he think such a thing?

Situation #2: No matter what you suggest, it feels like your boss always says something negative about your ideas. At first, you took it in stride. Then it made you so angry you fantasized about choking him for always putting you down. Eventually, you felt like something inside of you gave up.

You still have what you think are great ideas, but you rarely share them out loud. Instead, because you don't feel you receive the respect and appreciation you deserve, you entertain fits of seething bitterness.

You're still in your thirties, but a recent routine physical revealed that you are borderline for high blood pressure. Your doctor has given you a list of recommendations, none of which deals with what's going on inside your head and heart due to the stress and anxiety.

Situation #3: You're returning a product you purchased on Amazon at your local UPS Store. As you walk out, you make eye contact with a man seated against the wall just outside the door. He says, "Sir, I'm down on my luck and hungry. Could you spare me enough money to buy a decent meal?"

With indifference you say, "Sorry, friend, but I don't have any cash on me." As you walk to your car, you are overwhelmed with compassion and concern for this man. As you slide into the driver's seat, you remember that you have two water bottles in your car and feel prompted to give him, specifically, both bottles.

You walk back to the man and say, "I'm sorry I can't help with food, but here are a couple of water bottles." You sense his humiliation for being in need, but also his gratitude as he gulps it down. Suddenly you see what you had missed before. This man desperately needed something to drink.

That Conversation in Your Head Is a Lot More Than Self-Talk

We all know we carry on a running conversation with ourselves all day. We call it "self-talk."

We need self-talk to help us filter the bits and pieces of everyday life and forge them into a congruent story.

But our "self" is not the only voice in that conversation. Four other voices also constantly exert themselves to shape what we think, say, and do.

Every day when your feet hit the floor, three of these voices rail against the higher principles of your Christian faith. They are the root cause of hurt feelings, living to win the approval of others, not facing your problems like an adult, unforgiveness, holding grudges, oppressive and sad feelings, misinterpreting social cues, false guilt and shame, and generally feeling the weight of the world.

Fortunately, the fourth voice in your head, the Holy Spirit, is exponentially more powerful than the other three voices combined.

Everything you're about to learn, or be reminded of, can be distilled down to this idea:

> *The four voices in your head are the world, the flesh, the devil, and the Holy Spirit. Your job is to figure out which voice is speaking and take control of the conversation.*

The four voices in your head are the world, the flesh, the devil, and the Holy Spirit. Your job is to figure out which voice is speaking and take control of the conversation.

Understanding how to identify each of these voices and adjust the conversation is going to transform how you feel about getting up, starting your workday, going to the gym, making the most of your relationships with your spouse and children (if applicable), meeting with friends or strangers, your value as a person, facing challenges, and so many other situations.

What's at Stake

Unless and until you understand the four voices and how they work, you will continue to have inexplicable mood swings. You will continue to act out on your worst impulses and not know why. You will continue to be pleasant at work or school, but irritable around your family.

Until you know how to adjust what's going on in your head, you will experience ongoing frustration because you can't get control of your emotions. You will find yourself going to bed angry, waking in the middle of the night in a panic, getting up in the morning feeling exhausted, and then blindly repeating the cycle all over again.

Not mastering the voices in your head will eat away at your self-worth, poison your relationships, stunt your growth as a person, and limit how far you go in life.

So, before you blow up your relationship with your spouse, cuss out your boss, or send that emotionally charged email that's sitting in your outbox, let's figure out what's really going on and consider the higher principles that will help you master the narrative in your head.

We're going to devote an entire chapter to each of the four voices, but let's begin by briefly introducing each voice.

The Four Voices in Your Head

The first three voices will often overlap as this diagram illustrates:

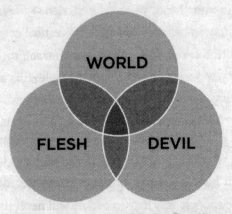

Diagram 1-1: The Overlap of the First Three Voices

But for our purposes, we're going to look at them individually so we can get a better understanding of how each voice works.

The World

The first voice is the world. Scripture tells us our world does not work in the way it did when God created it. You could say it's broken. In Christian terminology, it's "fallen." As a result, you will spend a lot of time managing the consequences of that brokenness. Colossians 2:8 cautions:

> *See to it that no one takes you captive through hollow and deceptive philosophy, which depends on human tradition and the elemental spiritual forces of this world rather than on Christ.*

What does the voice of the world sound like?

When I first started in business, I was told, "You have potential, but right now, you don't have enough gray hair so people will never listen to you." That was the voice of the world saying, "You're too young to make a difference."

But I've heard older men say they've been told, in so many words, "You're not useful anymore. You're expendable and you've been replaced, so we don't need you." That's the voice of the world saying, "You're too old."

As a result of sin, the world we live in is a juggernaut that relentlessly entices you to pursue life's riches and pleasures—and then crushes you for trying. Essentially, the voice of the fallen world wants you to think, *It doesn't matter if I'm young or old; I can't really make any difference.*

That's just one example of how "human tradition and the elemental spiritual forces of this world" try to turn the narrative inside your head into negative self-talk. We will explore the voice of the world further in the next chapter.

The Flesh

The second voice in your head is the flesh, or sinful nature. We all know we have it, but why? The Bible tells us our attraction to sinful desires has been a core element of human nature dating back to when Adam and Eve believed the devil's lies about God. Galatians 5:17 says:

> *For the flesh desires what is contrary to the Spirit, and the Spirit what is contrary to the flesh. They are in conflict with each other, so that you are not to do whatever you want.*

What does the voice of the flesh sound like?

While writing this book, I went through a blue period. I was feeling down, like things weren't going the way they're supposed to go. This went on for a few weeks.

What I was feeling inside had nothing to do with my wife, but eventually I twisted things around in my head enough to think, *It's her fault.*

This was hardly the first time I'd blamed her for something that had nothing to do with her. But before saying something I would regret, I took a few days to sort through what was really going on. I asked, "What does the voice of the Holy Spirit have to say about this?"

I had a double epiphany. First, because of my flesh and sinful nature, I often assume it's someone else's fault when something goes wrong. That's just arrogance, plain and simple.

The second epiphany was to realize no one in the whole world cares more about me than my wife. No one. She has always been there for me. She's the one person I can count on to help me when I'm feeling the weight of the world.

At that point, a metaphor popped to mind. I hope this can help you as much as it has helped me. I pictured us walking side-by-side. Suddenly, I stumbled, lost my balance, and started to go down. My wife reached out, took hold of my arm, and steadied me so that I didn't fall to the ground. In my mental picture, it was obvious she hadn't tripped me. I tripped on my own.

So, instead of blaming her, we sat down and I told her about my epiphanies—and all the ways I love and appreciate her so much. Then I told her about the metaphor and said, "Patsy, I've been stumbling for weeks, and I've lost my balance. I'm about to go down. I need you to reach out and grab my arm. Can you please help steady me so I don't fall to the ground?"

She did. And she was able to help me get to the bottom of what was really eating at me.

The Devil

The third voice in your head—the author of confusion and the tempter of your soul—is the devil. Is the devil real? Jesus certainly thought so. In John 8:44, Jesus said to some disbelieving people:

> *You belong to your father, the devil, and you want to carry out your father's desires. He was a murderer from the beginning, not holding to the truth, for there is no truth in him. When he lies, he speaks his native language, for he is a liar and the father of lies.*

Look again at how Jesus characterizes the devil: a murderer, no truth in him, lies are his native tongue, a liar, the father of lies.

Here's the bottom line: The devil wants to destroy what God wants to build.

What does the voice of the devil sound like?

The malware of choice for the devil is distrust, doubt, and despair. Once the devil hacks your brain and loads this malware onto your hard drive, it's a virus that spreads very quickly and turns into false guilt, false shame, and self-pity.

> The devil wants to destroy what God wants to build.

A man who attends The Man in the Mirror Bible Study did hard drugs for years. One day, he said, "I know God has forgiven me for all the terrible things I've done, but I'm having a hard time forgiving myself."

Strongly suspecting the voice of the devil was working on him, I asked, "So you believe God has forgiven you, right?"

"Yes."

"But you're having a hard time forgiving yourself, right?"

"Yes."

"So, what you're basically saying is that you have a higher standard for forgiveness than God. Is that right?"

The lightbulb went off, and he took another step down the road to recovery.

But that's how the voice of the devil works. He wants you to carry around the burden of what has already been forgiven. It really irks the devil when you accept the grace of our Lord and Savior Jesus Christ to take away the burden of all that shame and guilt—which brings us to the fourth voice.

The Holy Spirit

The Spirit brings calm to chaos, comfort to sorrow, peace to strife, clarity to confusion, and power to weakness. Jesus promised in John 14:26:

> But the Advocate, the Holy Spirit, whom
> the Father will send in my name, will
> teach you all things and will remind you
> of everything I have said to you.

What does the voice of the Spirit sound like? As my co-teacher at our Bible study, Khayree Pender, says, "If the words don't sound like the Holy Spirit, it's not Him!"

For example, let's take another look at how the world wants you to think: *It doesn't matter if I'm young or old, I can't really make any difference.*

The Holy Spirit tells a very different story through the Bible. Joseph, David, and Jesus all started their careers when they were 30 years of age, and we still feel their impact today.

Many of the most innovative ideas that shape our world start with men and women in their twenties, thirties, and early forties. Einstein introduced his theory of relativity when he was 26. Steve Jobs was 21 years old when he and Steve Wozniak started Apple in the Jobs' family garage. Rosa Parks was just 42 when she refused to give up her seat on a Montgomery, Alabama bus.

On the other hand, Scripture tells us that Sarah, Moses, Joshua, and Paul all did their best work in the last third of their lives. They were late bloomers. The book *Late Bloomers* features cameos of 75 people who made tremendous contributions in their later years—like Colonel Harland Sanders who first franchised Kentucky Fried Chicken at the age of 62.[1] And in both 2016 and 2020, America elected Presidents in their 70s.

As you can see, the Spirit wants you to hear the exact opposite of what the world wants you to hear. The Spirit wants you to know: "It doesn't matter how old you are, you can *always* make a difference."

The voice of the Spirit will empower you to keep the world on a leash, the flesh on house arrest, and the devil on a terrorist watch list.

These are the four voices affecting the conversation in our heads: the world, the flesh, the devil, and the Holy Spirit.

A Note on the Voices of Other People

While this is a book to help you master what's going on inside your own head, we need to say something about guarding against what's going on inside the heads of others.

My best friend, Jim, died seven years ago, but rarely a week goes by without me remembering a story about the repetitive cruelty of his father. When Jim was about 10 years old, he invited Timmy, his best friend from the neighborhood, over to his house to play. At the end of the day, as Timmy was about to leave, Jim's father heaped praise on Timmy in front of Jim, and then said, "Timmy, I sure wish I had a son like you."

> The voice of the Spirit will empower you to keep the world on a leash, the flesh on house arrest, and the devil on a terrorist watch list.

There are people we interact with who, wittingly and unwittingly, speak and act on behalf of the world, their own flesh, and the devil. In the parable of the wheat and weeds, Jesus talked about "people of the evil one" and said, "the enemy who sows them is the devil" (Matthew 13:38-39).

For example, when you are bullied, manipulated, cheated, abused, or subjected to false teaching—that's always sinful, often evil, and sometimes criminal. (It goes without saying that, if someone does something against you that rises to criminality, you should contact law enforcement immediately.)

When you recognize which of the four voices may be controlling other people, you can adjust your response. You can't control what others say and do, but with the help of the Spirit's voice you can take the high road through these painful encounters.

But even when we must take action to protect ourselves, we can still have sympathy for sinners, because we know that we all once "followed the ways of this *world* and of the *ruler of the kingdom of the air*… gratifying the cravings of our *flesh*" (Ephesians 2:2-3, emphasis added).

Notice all three of the negative voices are mentioned together in that one passage.

So, let's pray for them—"that they will come to their senses and escape from the trap of the devil, who has taken them captive to do his will" (2 Timothy 2:26).

For the purposes of this book, however, the mission is narrowed to the four voices fighting to control what's happening in our own minds.

You Can Take Control

Proverbs 4:23 says:

Above all else, guard your heart, for everything you do flows from it.

When a Bible passage begins with, "Above all else," that's like the jet flyover at the start of a race. Sit up, because what comes next is the main event.

Above all else—of all the things that could be said—Scripture isolates guarding your heart as a first principle.

What is the "heart"? Technically, the Hebrew word for heart is *leb* and includes the intellect, will, and emotions—all the things that establish your individual identity.

Today, we're more likely to say "mind" than "heart," but the idea is the same. It's the totality of our inner being. And the Bible says, "above all else," guard *that*.

Why does the Bible put such extreme emphasis on guarding your heart? Because, as the verse continues, "everything you do flows from it." Other Bible versions say: "for it determines the course of your life" (NLT), and "that's where life starts" (MSG).

Your heart is the starting point for every thought you think, every word you speak, and every action you take.

Guarding the heart is such a big issue because our hearts (minds) are so vulnerable to being hacked or burglarized.

What would an unguarded heart look like? An unguarded heart might look like an unguarded house.

In our neighborhood, we've had a few burglaries over the years. My wife and I have taken steps to protect ourselves.

If someone knocks on the door, we don't automatically open it. We keep our windows locked. We have floodlights on sensors. We have an alarm system with monitoring. I spent about $100 and bought some video cameras, so we also have video surveillance. I put a light on a timer in one of the front rooms that turns on at dusk and off around midnight, hopefully to confuse a burglar who might be casing the place. I installed a fake TV device that makes it look like somebody's home watching TV when it's dark outside and the curtains are closed.

> What would an unguarded heart look like? An unguarded heart might look like an unguarded house.

Then there's our yappy little dog who goes berserk when anyone steps onto our property, literally bouncing off furniture while racing from window to window. I'm still startled and flinch every time she lets loose with that shrill, high-pitched bark. If I was a burglar, I would probably laugh at a dog that sounds like it swallowed a squeaky toy, but I would still run away as fast as I could!

Even if a burglar did get past all those safeguards, they would be in for a big surprise. My wife doesn't have jewelry, we don't have art, and whatever papers we have of any value are locked up in a safe deposit box.

We've been intentional to take the obvious, logical, and practical steps to guard our house. And that's exactly what God is telling us to do with our hearts.

God would not tell you, "Above all else, guard your heart," if He could not also equip you to do it.

God would not tell you, "Above all else, guard your heart," if He could not also equip you to do it.

Just like you might guard your house from unwanted intruders, there are intentional steps you can take to guard your heart.

Making the Adjustment

To that end, chapters 2 through 5 each conclude with a "Making the Adjustment" section, which will equip you with a cumulative set of spiritual disciplines, habits, and virtues that can help you guard your heart and take control.

Here's a diagram with a preview, and you can also view the full list in Appendix 1: Making the Adjustment Summary Chart:

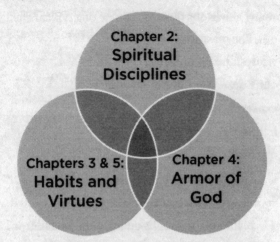

Diagram 1-2: Compilation of Spiritual Disciplines, Habits, Virtues, and Practices

In addition, I've included "Reflection and Discussion" questions at the end of each chapter to help you begin making adjustments right away. Here's an exercise to help you get started.

QUICK START EXERCISE

This Quick Start Exercise will help you understand which voices are loudest in your head for many situations over the course of a typical day.

The main point of the exercise isn't precision. It's designed simply to get you thinking about how the four voices influence you in everyday life.

Go ahead and give it a try.

Step 1. In the *State of Mind* column below, write down your normal state of mind for each applicable *Situation* listed. For example, you could write:

> glad, sad, mad, bad, hurt, moody, fragile, bruised, fearful, concerned, anxious, frustrated, out of control, impatient, irritable, prickly, feeling superior or inferior, competent or incompetent, shame, guilt, needed, unneeded, wanted, unwanted, loved, unloved, understood, misunderstood, useful, not useful, used, appreciated, underappreciated, melancholy, self-pity, bitter, lustful,

greedy, jealous, envious, covetous, happy, joyful, at peace.

Step 2. Next, take a guess at which voice is most likely responsible for each state of mind you identified: the world, the flesh, the devil, or the Holy Spirit. Write your answers in the *Voice* column. Again, this is a "get-acquainted" exercise, so don't be concerned about precision.

As a sample, I've filled out the chart for the three situations included at the beginning of this chapter:

SITUATION:	STEP 1: *State of Mind*	STEP 2: *Voice*
Brad at small group	sad, used	devil
Around unappreciative boss	bitter, undervalued	flesh
Meeting man's need for a drink	joyful, moved	Spirit

Now you try it:

SITUATION: *The last time you...*	STEP 1: *State of Mind*	STEP 2: *Voice*
Got out of bed		
Were criticized for your work		
Got home from work		
Spent time on social media		
Exercised		
Argued with your spouse		
Connected with your spouse		
Saw your child excel or rebel		

SITUATION: *The last time you...*	STEP 1: *State of Mind*	STEP 2: *Voice*
Were cheered up by a friend		
Were let down by a friend		
Read the Bible		
Spent time praying		
Went to church		
Woke up during the night		
Thought about your purpose		
Caught up on the news		
Thought about the state of the world		

Throughout the next chapters, we're going to more fully explore how you can better recognize the four voices and make any needed adjustments. As you begin to practice taking control of your thoughts, God is going to honor your desire. He will help you sharpen your ability to figure out which voice is speaking and, when necessary, bring your responses into alignment with the voice of His Spirit.

A Personal Prayer

Our dearest Father, thank You for revealing the different voices that influence the conversation in our heads and hearts in Scripture. Help each of us to understand that the four voices in our heads are the world, the flesh, the devil, and the Holy Spirit. As we proceed, teach us to discern which voices are speaking so we can take control of the conversation. Grant us wisdom to sort out our thoughts so we can walk in the fullness of Your presence and power. We ask this in Jesus' name. Amen.

In the next chapter, let's explore how you can gain the upper hand on the voice of the world. But first answer these questions.

Reflection and Discussion

NOTE: If in a small group, share your answers with each other. To start and lead a group, see Appendix 2, "How to Lead a Discussion Group."

1. If you have not already done so, complete the Quick Start Exercise. What was your biggest surprise?

2. What are the four voices? Why is it important to figure out which voice is speaking and make the adjustment, according to Proverbs 4:23, cited on page 22?

3. Describe your most prevalent mood or state of mind. For example, you could answer one of the following: confused, overwhelmed, anxious, fearful, sad, numb, easily offended, irritable, angry, ready to explode, joyful, peaceful, content, or filled with love. What have you already read that can help you take control of what's going on in your head?

TWO

The Voice of the World

Do not conform to the pattern of this world, but be transformed by the renewing of your mind. Then you will be able to test and approve what God's will is—his good, pleasing and perfect will.

Romans 12:2

French mathematician and theologian Blaise Pascal (1623-1662) said, "All men seek happiness. There are no exceptions... This is the motive of every action of every man, including those who go and hang themselves."[2]

To illustrate his point, Pascal went on to explain that one man goes to war while another man stays home, but they both do it for the same reason—they think that's what will make them happy.

Every person in the world tries to move his or her life forward. We all want to make something of ourselves and find our lot in life so we can be happy.

Solomon put it like this: "I know that there is *nothing better* for people than to be happy and to do good while they live" (Ecclesiastes 3:12, emphasis added). The words "nothing better" compare to the words "above all else" in the previous chapter. They're like the national anthem just before the jet flyover.

> We all want to make something of ourselves and find our lot in life so we can be happy.

But most of us also say, "It's just hard."

Why is life so hard? Scripture warns that the world is not our friend. In this chapter, you will learn (or be reminded) what Scripture means by "the world," how the voice of the world tries to get inside your head, and how you can keep it out.

You may or may not change the world, but you don't have to let the world change you.

What Happened to the World?

According to Genesis 1, God created the world and saw that it was not only good, but very good. However, the introduction of sin into the human race by Adam and Eve threw the world into the perpetual struggle between good and evil we see depicted in every form of art, literature, film, and news.

While the specific struggles in "the pattern of this world" are always changing, what doesn't change is the ever-present brokenness because of the fall.

Today's fallen world is scarred with broken relationships, fatherlessness, chronic pain, addictions, security guards in schools, pandemics, poverty, racism, sexual violence, human trafficking, abortion, elder fraud, online bullying, mass shootings, wars, corruption, gender confusion, and more.

> You may or may not change the world, but you don't have to let the world change you.

As bleak as that sounds, as twentieth century theologian Francis Schaeffer said, "There is still a lot of leftover beauty in the world."[3] Leftover beauty from God's initial creation surrounds us from the crimson sunset that thrills your senses, the majesty of mountains that conjure up thoughts about how big God must be, the loving thoughts evoked by watching a precious family on a picnic in the park, and the way a mother duck cares for her baby ducks.

Plus, human achievement across a broad spectrum is nothing short of spectacular: medical advancements, space exploration, smart phones, democracy, agricultural production, reducing poverty for almost one billion people, electric cars, and so much more.

What, then, is going on? When the apostle Paul wrote, "Do not conform any longer to the pattern of this world," he meant the pattern of the *fallen* world—not the leftover beauty or human achievement.

How then does the fallen world—in its brokenness—attract us?

This fallen world woos us with the combined voice of all the philosophies, beliefs, and worldviews that have evolved over the centuries that encourage people to do what seems right in their own eyes.

Any worldview that "suppresses the truth" about God is part of the pattern of this world (see Romans 1:18-19). That includes any philosophy or belief system that puts *self* at the center, whether you call it materialism, hedonism, secularism, nihilism, narcissism, or the prosperity gospel.

The fallen world is where the flesh and devil have wreaked their havoc. The fallen world has broken ranks with God's "very good" plan. That's the world we are talking about in this chapter.

How the World Is Trying to Get Inside Your Head

Whatever you're pursuing—whether significance, personal autonomy, meaning, money, power, career success, love, or faith in Jesus Christ— you're doing so because you think it will ultimately make you happy.

The voice of the world wants you to believe,

It's going to take a lot more than Jesus Christ to make me happy.

But may I ask, has listening to the world's voice ever produced any lasting peace, happiness, or contentment for you? Rather, doesn't it tap into your worst insecurities and leave you feeling discontent?

Consider Derrick. Derrick grew up in church, but when he went to college, he became enamored with all the latest fads about how to find a good life. He came to believe, *Money will solve my problems. Success will make me happy. A dynamic career will give me meaning. And as a Christian, I can have the best of both worlds.*

> The voice of the world wants you to believe, *It's going to take a lot more than Jesus Christ to make me happy.*

Unfortunately, deep inside his brain, there was a coding error. Like Jesus said, "No one can serve two masters" (see Luke 16:13).

Fortunately for Derrick, he was never able to find what he was looking for by serving two masters, and he finally returned to the faith of his youth.

But it begs the question, how did the world lure Derrick to look elsewhere for happiness in the first place? And, of course, how does the world lure *us*?

The biblical explanation found in Romans 1:20-25 tells us that, although God's invisible qualities have been clearly seen from the beginning of the world, people don't honor Him as God or give Him thanks. As a result, they become *wise in their own eyes.*

Like a curious dog always pulling against the end of the leash, they want to try out all the trending ideas about how to find contentment and satisfaction. They end up exchanging God's glory for idols and trading the truth about God for this lie:

> *"Jesus Christ alone is not enough to make me happy. I need something else."*

And, to those like Derrick who lack spiritual wisdom and maturity, doing what seems right in their own eyes *does* make them quite happy—at least, in the beginning.

For an example of how "the pattern of this world" gets inside your head, consider sex outside of marriage, which has become far less controversial than in the past.

Even though the Bible is unambiguous about sex outside of marriage, Pew Research reports 85% of Americans think that it's fine for a man and a woman to live together in a sexual relationship and not be married. In fact, 69% of them think that it's okay even if they never plan to get married.[4]

Sex outside of marriage is a bad idea for many well-documented health reasons, but what really matters is that it's a sin. But the world's voice has so permeated our culture that you will sound like a complete dinosaur—hopelessly old-fashioned and out of touch—if you openly agree with the Bible.

> *It turns out, the world doesn't mind if you become a Christian, as long as you keep living like you're not.*

Once the fallen world's voice gets inside your head, it can seduce you to dismiss or wink at many similar biblical principles.

It turns out, the world doesn't mind if you become a Christian, as long as you keep living like you're not.

Why Doesn't God Just Fix the Broken World?

We've all wondered, *If Jesus Christ could fix the world, why hasn't He done it yet?*

That's a fair question, but it misses the point of Jesus' purpose. Jesus did not come to fix the world. He did not come to reverse the fall or to restore the fallen world to its pre-fallen state. Jesus did not come to help people build their kingdoms.

Jesus Christ came "to seek and to save the lost" (Luke 19:10). Jesus said, "My kingdom is not of this world…. my kingdom is from another place" (John 18:36).

That doesn't mean we shouldn't work for the betterment of this world. Jesus certainly did. He healed the sick. He fed the poor. He loved and cared about everyone from a rich young ruler to a woman caught in adultery.

So, by all means, let's try to find solutions for racial injustice, sexual violence, and human trafficking. By all means, let's work for peace and prosperity in the communities where we live.

However, restoring the world to its pre-fallen state is not what the gospel is all about. Rather, the gospel helps us make sense of our world, and then it gives us hope through faith in Jesus Christ.

The Serenity Prayer, famously used in Alcoholics Anonymous, is part of a longer poem by twentieth century theologian Reinhold Niebuhr. The poem begins with the familiar part:

> God, give me the serenity to accept the things I cannot change,
> the courage to change the things that should be changed, and
> the wisdom to know the difference.

His poem goes on to say:

> Living one day at a time,
> enjoying one moment at a time,
> accepting hardship as a pathway to peace,
> taking, as Jesus did, this sinful world as it is,

not as I would have it.
Trusting that You will make all things
right, if I surrender to Your will,
that I may be reasonably happy in this
life, and
supremely happy with You forever in the
next. [5]

The world says, "I can make you happy by
giving you whatever seems right in your own
eyes." But the truth of the gospel is that you will
never find true happiness and contentment in this
world apart from God.

What Does the Voice of the World Sound Like in Your Head?

Colossians 2:8 says:

*See to it that no one takes you captive
through hollow and deceptive philosophy, which depends on human tradition
and the elemental spiritual forces of this
world rather than on Christ.*

If you are taken "captive," that means you're a prisoner, enslaved by your captor. Our minds will be taken captive by the "hollow and deceptive" forces if we can't recognize the sound of the world's voice.

For example, almost everything Nathan reads online, watches in his shows, and sees happening to his friends, shouts, "Divorce is no big deal." Like all couples, he and his wife have had some challenges. But even though Nathan has faith in God, he struggles with whether he should fight for his marriage or just get a divorce. Why? Because his mind has been taken hostage by the world's voice telling him, "You deserve to be free. You deserve to be happy. It's time to move on."

But the world's voice is 25,000 miles wide and an inch deep, because the world's voice downplays the importance of values like commitment, sacrifice, humility, loyalty, serving each other, and the difficult tasks of communicating and resolving conflicts.

The underlying message of the world's voice today, blared through an onslaught of round-the-clock news, entertainment, and social media, is that what will *really* make you happy are, for example:

- *Freedom:* I deserve the freedom to do whatever I want, whenever, wherever, and with whomever. I'm tired of all the rules.

- *Fame:* I want to be famous for something—anything. Then people will like me. Then I will be okay.

- *Fortune:* I want to strike it rich—that's something worth giving my life to. Money will definitely make me happy.

- *Feel-Good Spirituality:* God just wants me to be happy.

- *Personal Truth:* There isn't one right way or one truth. Truth is relative. What matters is that I find *my* truth.

- *Performance:* My worth is determined by my performance. I need to prove to the world I'm good enough. If it's going to be, it's up to me.

- ***Personal Peace:*** That's not my problem. I don't want to get involved. I just want to be left alone so I can do my own thing. I paid my dues, and now it's my turn.

How to Keep the World Out of Your Head

How can you keep the world out of your head? Scripture gives us the guidance we need to make the adjustment. Reflect on your own relationship to the fallen world as you read these verses:

> *Do not love the world or anything in the world. If anyone loves the world, love for the Father is not in them. (1 John 2:15)*

> *Do not conform to the pattern of this world, but be transformed by the renewing of your mind. Then you will be able to test and approve what God's will is—his good, pleasing and perfect will. (Romans 12:2)*

We demolish arguments and every pretension that sets itself up against the knowledge of God, and we take captive every thought to make it obedient to Christ. (2 Corinthians 10:5)

From now on…those who use the things of the world (should live) as if not engrossed in them. For this world in its present form is passing away. (1 Corinthians 7:29, 31, parenthetic comment added)

Anyone who chooses to be a friend of the world becomes an enemy of God. (James 4:4)

What did you learn about yourself from these verses? The bottom line is that we can take control over the world's voice by letting God's word continually renew our minds so that we are:

- Not taken captive by hollow and deceptive philosophy
- Not loving the world

- Not conformed to the pattern of this world
- Able to know God's will
- Taking every thought captive to make it obedient to Christ
- Not engrossed with the things of the world
- Not becoming a friend of the world

Jesus has left us *in* the world, but we are not *of* the world (John 17:11, 14). That's because the world is not our real home.

We are aliens and strangers in this world. We are pilgrims, just passing through. As Jesus promised, "I will come back and take you to be with me that you also may be where I am" (John 14:3).

Affirming that Christ Is Enough to Make Us Happy

Once I was speaking at a prayer breakfast in Great Falls, Montana. A man pressed a small sheet of yellow paper into my hand and walked away. Later when I opened it, I was moved. It said,

I have enough. I am enough.

Those are words to live by. Is Jesus Christ enough for you? Or do you think you need something else to be happy?

As you read Ephesians 2:1-9 below, I invite you to humbly and fully embrace

> *I have enough.*
> *I am enough.*

Jesus, whether it's for the first time or an act of renewal, affirming that He is enough.

> *As for you, you were dead in your transgressions and sins, in which you used to live when you followed the ways of this world and of the ruler of the kingdom of the air, the spirit who is now at work in those who are disobedient.*
>
> *All of us also lived among them at one time, gratifying the cravings of our flesh and following its desires and thoughts. Like the rest, we were by nature deserving of wrath.*

But because of his great love for us, God, who is rich in mercy, made us alive with Christ even when we were dead in transgressions—it is by grace you have been saved. And God raised us up with Christ and seated us with him in the heavenly realms in Christ Jesus, in order that in the coming ages he might show the incomparable riches of his grace, expressed in his kindness to us in Christ Jesus.

For it is by grace you have been saved, through faith—and this is not from yourselves, it is the gift of God—not by works, so that no one can boast.

The voice of the world wants to convince you, "It's going to take a lot more than Jesus Christ to make you happy."

But as the first sentence in the passage above says, when we tried to find happiness by following the ways of this world, we were spiritually dead. Not just comatose. *Dead.*

The gospel, on the other hand, says that because of His great love, God has made you *alive with Christ*.

And so, here's the question: Is that enough for you?

If you've never professed faith in this good news before, or if you want to renew or reaffirm your faith, let me encourage you to do that now. You can simply pray:

> *Jesus, thank You for your great love and mercy. I confess my sins and by faith, through your grace, I ask You to be my Savior and Lord both now and forever, and that will be enough for me. Amen.*

If you have struggled with the voices in your head and heart, putting your faith in Jesus Christ is the important first step and foundation to everything that follows. So, congratulations and welcome, or welcome back, to the kingdom of Christ.

Making the Adjustment
Spiritual Disciplines to Hear
from God

The world's voice is determined to influence the story you tell yourself and live out. Now it's time to show how you can start making adjustments to that story and take back control of the conversation. Here is a set of tools to help turn down the noise volume so you can more clearly hear from God.

1. The Bible:
What Does the Bible Say?

Anytime you feel confused or uncertain, the single most important question to ask is, "Has God already spoken on this matter?"

The Bible is chock full of *commands* (which are duty) and *principles* (which are wise) to guide you.

For example, because of God's word, we don't have to wonder if it's okay to not report $1,800 of incidental income to the IRS. The Bible is clear about lying, cheating, stealing, and submitting to those in authority (Romans 13:1-6).

Or, consider the man who said God called him to be a missionary in China. His wife didn't want to go, so he divorced her and went anyway. That's just mixed up—which is why it's important to know God will never lead in contradiction to His written word.

The Bible has a plan for your success. It's for you to delight in God's word and meditate on it continually throughout your waking hours:

Anytime you feel confused or uncertain, the single most important question to ask is, "Has God already spoken on this matter?"

Blessed is the one who does not walk in step with the wicked or stand in the way that sinners take or sit in the company of mockers, but whose delight is in the law of the LORD, and who meditates on his law day and night. That person is like a tree planted by streams of water, which yields its fruit in season and whose leaf does not wither—whatever they do prospers. (Psalm 1:1-3)

God's word will help you see yourself with a clarity you will never achieve any other way:

> *For the word of God is alive and active. Sharper than any double-edged sword, it penetrates even to dividing soul and spirit, joints and marrow; it judges the thoughts and attitudes of the heart. (Hebrews 4:12)*

2. Prayer:
How Is God Leading Me in Prayer?

Over and over, Scripture invites us to present our requests to God:

> *For we do not have a high priest who is unable to empathize with our weaknesses, but we have one who has been tempted in every way, just as we are—yet he did not sin. Let us then approach God's throne of grace with confidence, so that we may receive mercy and find grace to help us in our time of need. (Hebrews 4:15-16)*

Do not be anxious about anything, but in every situation, by prayer and petition, with thanksgiving, present your requests to God. And the peace of God, which transcends all understanding, will guard your hearts and your minds in Christ Jesus. (Philippians 4:6-7)

Simply put, God promises to answer prayer. If you are still roiling inside about what to do, it's doubtful God has answered your prayer yet, so keep praying. Peace is the umpire.

3. The Holy Spirit: What Is the Spirit Saying?

God lives in us in the person of the Holy Spirit. "Don't you know that you yourselves are God's temple and that God's Spirit dwells in your midst?" (1 Corinthians 3:16).

What is the role of the Holy Spirit? He is our counselor, helper, comforter, advocate, encourager, and power. "But the Advocate, the Holy Spirit, whom the Father will send in my name, will teach you all things and will remind you of everything I have said to you" (John 14:26).

Consciously depend on Him, and He will both guide you and intercede for you. "The Spirit intercedes for God's people in accordance with the will of God" (Romans 8:27). Chapter Five will explain how to hear the Spirit's voice.

4. Conscience:
What Does My Conscience Say?

We must always live by the pledge of a good conscience toward God and other people. That's obvious. However, while a guilty conscience provides clear evidence you are not in God's will, a clear conscience may not guarantee you have correctly discerned God's will. Paul said, "My conscience is clear, but that does not make me innocent. It is the Lord who judges me" (1 Corinthians 4:4).

Ricardo filed for divorce abruptly one day after several difficult years of marriage. He told his friend, "I have peace about this. My conscience is clear." His friend paused and then said, "Don't mistake your human relief for God's peace."

Conscience is more effective as a red light than a green light. To go against conscience is neither wise nor safe. On the other hand, "If our hearts do not condemn us, we have confidence before God" (1 John 3:21).

5. Circumstances: What Do Circumstances Suggest?

Some people are born short, some tall. Some in America, some in Argentina. Some to poor parents, some to rich. God's will is often revealed clearly by the circumstances in which we live. "He marked out their appointed times in history and the boundaries of their lands" (Acts 17:26).

How does this apply when we're trying to hear from God in our daily lives?

If you want to purchase a house that will require a $200,000 mortgage and you can only qualify for $150,000, then your circumstances have told you God's will.

Or take the example of Jason, a single father of two young children. After months of prayer, money, and work, Jason's custody case didn't go as he hoped. Although he felt devastated, he shared, "I spent months praying for God's will to be done. This is not how I hoped it would go or what *I* think is best for the kids, but God must know something I don't, because I have to believe He answered my prayers and—for now—this *is* His will."

6. Counsel: What Are My Counselors Telling Me?

Often, we just need a good listener to help us crystallize our thoughts into coherent words. Other times, we need the advice of a trusted friend.

Proverbs 15:22 says: "Plans fail for lack of counsel, but with many advisers they succeed."

You should regularly seek out counsel, but make sure the counsel is coming from someone who sincerely wants to help you find God's will. If not, you will only add to the confusion in your heart and mind.

7. Fasting: Should I Fast About This?

Sometimes the pattern of this world has such a vice grip on the story we've been telling ourselves that we need a tangible interruption. Fasting provides it.

Jesus talked about fasting as a common practice in the Sermon on the Mount in Matthew 6:16-18. Worship, prayer, and fasting are often linked together in the Bible, and the apostle Paul included fasting before making major decisions.

The reason to fast is that it slows down our physical functions so that our minds can be more in tune with Christ. Fasting demonstrates a seriousness about our concern to the Lord.

There's no one way to fast. If you're new to fasting, you could start by skipping a meal and spending that time praying instead. Personally, I regularly do a 24-hour fast that skips two meals, but I drink a couple of protein drinks for energy. I will do my normal work but devote an hour or so to prayer sometime during those 24 hours.

You might also consider fasting from social media, your shows, or anything else that makes you feel overly dependent.

These seven disciplines—the Bible, prayer, the Holy Spirit, conscience, circumstances, counsel and fasting—will help train your mind to defend against the world's seductive voice.

Do them only occasionally, and it will amount to nothing more than priming a rusty pump. Do them regularly, and you will hear God's will as clearly as if He sent you a voice text.

A Personal Prayer

Our dearest Father, thank You for your Scripture. Thank You for the affirmation that You have come not to fix the broken world, but rather to bring Your gospel to us, so that we might be liberated from our bondage to decay and death. Lord, when the world says, "It's going to take a lot more than Jesus Christ to make you happy," give us the ability to reject that thought, because we have guarded our hearts above all else. We ask this in Jesus' name. Amen.

Reflection and Discussion

1. The voice of the fallen world tries to get inside your head by luring you to want and worry about (or dismiss) many things. Which of the following "hollow and deceptive philosophies" and "patterns of this world" are trying to take you captive, and with what result? Check as many as apply:

____*Freedom:* I deserve the freedom to do whatever I want, whenever, wherever, and with whomever. I'm tired of all the rules.

____*Fame:* I want to be famous for something—anything.

____*Fortune:* I want to strike it rich—that's something worth giving my life to.

____*Feel-Good Spirituality:* God just wants me to be happy.

____*Relative Truth:* There isn't one right way or one truth. What matters is that I find *my* truth.

____*Personal Peace:* I just want to be left alone so I can do my own thing and look out for myself. I paid my dues, and now it's my turn.

____*Other:* _____

_____

2. Based on the Scriptures in the section "How to Keep the World Out of Your Head," what is the most important thing you've learned, or been reminded of, about the voice of the world?

3. I highly recommend you memorize these seven questions from Making the Adjustment so that you can run through them whenever the will of God doesn't seem clear. Refer back to the statement(s) you checked in Question #1 as trying to take you captive, and ask yourself:

The Bible: What does the Bible say?

_____

_____

Prayer: How is God leading me in prayer?

_____

_____

The Holy Spirit: What is the Spirit saying?

_____

_____

Conscience: What does my conscience say?

_____

_____

Circumstances: What do circumstances suggest?

_____

_____

Counsel: What are my counselors telling me?

_____

_____

Fasting: Should I fast about this?

_____

_____

THREE

The Voice of the Flesh

*For the flesh desires what is contrary
to the Spirit, and the Spirit what is
contrary to the flesh. They are
in conflict with each other, so that
you are not to do whatever you want.*

Galatians 5:17

One day, I was working on this chapter. I opted to take a break downstairs—my office is over the garage—and while I was away from my desk, I had an idea for the book I didn't want to forget. I stopped what I was doing, intending to rush back upstairs so I could write it down.

My wife was lounging on the couch, catching up online. I thought it was obvious I was in a hurry as I swept by her, but nevertheless, she said, "Honey, could you get me another cup of coffee?"

I froze for five full speechless seconds, conflicted over whether to respond in my flesh or in the Spirit.

Hopefully it wasn't just because I was working on this chapter on how to defeat the voice of the flesh, but I did say, "Of course! I'd be happy to get you another cup of coffee."

So, I poured her another coffee—my highest and best use. Then I rushed back upstairs to write down my idea which was, frankly, insignificant compared to serving my wife.

> *I froze for five full speechless seconds, conflicted over whether to respond in my flesh or in the Spirit.*

Okay, so that's a time I successfully listened to the voice of the Spirit. But sometimes I do respond in the flesh. We all do. Why? Because, as Paul said of himself, "So I find this law at work: Although I want to do good, evil is right there with me" (Romans 7:21). And therein lies the problem.

The Greek word for "the flesh" is often translated "the sinful nature." The flesh is the dark side of our human nature. It's our baser instincts, our ever-present propensity to sin. The Scriptures variously refer to our fallen nature as:

- the flesh
- the sinful nature
- the cravings of the sinful nature
- the passions and desires of the flesh
- the law of sin and death
- another law in me waging war
- the desires that battle within

Of course, some people are bent on evil, but the vast majority of us, like Paul, want to do good. Yet even the kindest, most gentle person has secret sinful thoughts that sometimes spill out.

This chapter will explain why we keep sinning. It will help identify what triggers your own sinful cravings and suggest seven practical habits and virtues that can help you manage against the voice of the flesh.

Why Do We Keep Sinning?

To answer the question, "Why do we keep sinning?" we turn again to the heart (mind). Jesus taught:

> What comes out of a person is what defiles them. For it is from within, out of a person's heart, that evil thoughts come—sexual immorality, theft, murder, adultery, greed, malice, deceit, lewdness, envy, slander, arrogance and folly. All these evils come from inside and defile a person. (Mark 7:20-23)

> For whatever is in your heart determines what you say. (Matthew 12:34, NLT)

The prophet Jeremiah said:

> The heart is deceitful above all things and beyond cure. (Jeremiah 17:9)

We all feel the incurability of this deceit, don't we? I've always loved a nice car. One day, I was driving next to a car that looked almost identical to mine, but not as nice. For a split second, I felt deceptively "better" than the owner of that other car. I instantly repented, but that's how rapidly the deceitfulness of the flesh can overpower. How is that kind of sin still possible after decades of walking with Jesus?

The reason we keep sinning is that we have a dual nature. In fact, if you are a believer, you also have a third nature.

First, creation made you an image of God— the *high* you. Second, the fall made you "like the beasts"[4]—the *low* you. Third, faith in Jesus makes you a "new creation"—the *new* you.

> *Therefore, if anyone is in Christ, the new creation has come: The old has gone, the new is here!" (2 Corinthians 5:17)*

Our conversion to a new creation, however, is both an *event* and a *process*—the event of salvation and the lifelong process of sanctification.

Augustine wrote that when you were in your natural state, you were "not able to not sin." He also wrote that in heaven, you will "not be able to sin." But in this life, in your new creation nature, you are "able to sin or to not sin."

> *Even Paul, who wrote a third of the New Testament, told us that he, too, personally battled with his flesh.*

That ability to sin or to not sin—free will—is what creates the spiritual battle within us all. Even Paul, who wrote a third of the New Testament, told us that he, too, personally battled with his flesh:

> *I do not understand what I do. For what I want to do I do not do, but what I hate I do.*
>
> *And if I do what I do not want to do, I agree that the law is good. As it is, it is no longer I myself who do it, but it is sin living in me.*
>
> *For I know that good itself does not dwell in me, that is, in my sinful nature. For I have the desire to do what is good, but I cannot carry it out.*

For I do not do the good I want to do, but the evil I do not want to do—this I keep on doing. Now if I do what I do not want to do, it is no longer I who do it, but it is sin living in me that does it.

So I find this law at work: Although I want to do good, evil is right there with me. For in my inner being I delight in God's law; but I see another law at work in me, waging war against the law of my mind and making me a prisoner of the law of sin at work within me.

What a wretched man I am! Who will rescue me from this body that is subject to death? Thanks be to God, who delivers me through Jesus Christ our Lord! So then, I myself in my mind am a slave to God's law, but in my sinful nature a slave to the law of sin. (Romans 7:15-25)

What can we take away from this powerful passage? Paul helps us see that the believer's struggle with sin is the normal Christian experience.

Sin is buried deep inside you. You are not the villain. Sin is the villain. And Jesus Christ can be your hero.

An illustration may help. In our yard, we have a large oak tree. An invasive vine, cat's claw, keeps growing up the side of the tree, and I keep pulling it off. Left unchecked, the cat's claw would climb fifty feet and cover much of the tree.

Paul helps us see that the believer's struggle with sin is the normal Christian experience.

Why don't I just pull it out by the roots? I would like to, but it has a bulbous root that has become embedded in the roots of the tree. The only way to get rid of the vine would be to cut out so much of the roots that I would kill the tree. So instead, I manage the problem by pulling off new shoots of the vine when they appear.

In a similar way, the sinful nature is buried so deep within us that it can't be completely removed. It has to be managed.

Identify What Triggers
Your Sinful Cravings

The types of sinful cravings we hear from the flesh are limitless, but most of what we hear fits into one of three "dialects":

> For everything in the world—**the lust of the flesh, the lust of the eyes, and the pride of life**—comes not from the Father but from the world. (1 John 2:16, emphasis added)

Let's explore how the voice of the flesh tries to get in your head using these three dialects.

1. The Lust of the Flesh

When you think of the lust of the flesh, the first thing that probably comes to mind is sexual temptation. And for good reason—the Bible is clear that the risk is great:

> Flee from sexual immorality. All other sins a person commits are outside the body, but whoever sins sexually, sins against their own body. Do you not

know that your bodies are temples of the
Holy Spirit, who is in you, whom you
have received from God? You are not
your own; you were bought at a price.
Therefore honor God with your bodies.
(1 Corinthians 6:18-20)

Michael's battle with sexual temptation began at the age of 12 years old when he stumbled on several adult magazines in his father's closet. His head began to spin as he looked at the pictures. He did not flee. In fact, through his teen years he became a self-described addict. Today, he is a recovering addict, but as he says, "Those images are hard to erase."

Job gave us a principle to thwart sexual temptation. He said: "I made a covenant with my eyes not to look lustfully at a young woman" (Job 31:1).

Sexual temptations, however, are not the only things that trigger the lust of our flesh. Lust, by definition, indicates an intense, unbridled longing.

All sensual desires promise to make you feel good, happy, or anesthetize your pain. The pleasures of food, for example, when used to soothe

the pain in your heart can create innumerable health problems. And the tragic outcomes of drug or alcohol abuse need no further explanation.

What is it for you? In what ways are you vulnerable to the voice of the flesh triggering your sinful cravings? It's not easy to admit, is it?

2. The Lust of the Eyes

Blake is the first member of his family to earn a college degree. After bouncing around for a few years of underemployment, he was hired as a salesperson for a publishing company. Having seen how the love of money had corrupted his parents, Blake swore he was going to be different.

Blake was not only a great salesman but excelled at helping his peers maximize their potential. Just four years after starting at his company, 31-year-old Blake was appointed vice president of sales.

Blake succeeded in his goal to not make money his idol. Instead, he found his happiness by creating a high-performance organization. Success, performance, and results trumped every other value. As the years went by, he began to view his salespeople, authors, and customers as merely a means to these ends. If you underperformed, he cut you off.

> *The lust of the eyes cannot be satisfied: "I want more, more, more."*

Blake did not succumb to the love of money, but the flesh came at him from a different direction. Now he tramples over people to get what he wants. Worldly ambition is his hustle—his drug of choice.

The lust of the eyes includes out-of-control desires for success, money, position, power, experiences, and possessions. The lust of the eyes cannot be satisfied: "I want more, more, more."

In what ways are you vulnerable to the voice of the flesh triggering the greed inherent in your sinful nature?

3. The Pride of Life

The third dialect of the flesh is the pride of life. Pride wants to get the glory, receive the praise, and

THE VOICE OF THE FLESH

win the worship. Pride looks down on others with judgment or up at others with jealously. Pride is arrogant and independent, rejecting the advice of others and insisting on its own way. Pride is the critical spirit that holds others to a standard we ourselves can't or won't keep.

The pride of life is no respecter of persons. The poor are just as susceptible as the rich, and the righteous as vulnerable as the unrighteous. In fact, the more righteous you become in your own eyes, the more likely you are to fall into the pride of life.

> *Pride is the critical spirit that holds others to a standard we ourselves can't or won't keep.*

This may seem counterintuitive, but we've all known religious people who got "too big for their britches."

Jesus, too, was deeply concerned about religious hypocrites. We see this play out in a story he told about a Pharisee and a tax collector who both went to the temple to pray. It's best savored in Jesus' own words:

"Two men went up to the temple to pray, one a Pharisee and the other a tax collector. The Pharisee stood by himself and prayed: 'God, I thank you that I am not like other people—robbers, evildoers, adulterers—or even like this tax collector. I fast twice a week and give a tenth of all I get.'

"But the tax collector stood at a distance. He would not even look up to heaven, but beat his breast and said, 'God, have mercy on me, a sinner.'

"I tell you that this man, rather than the other, went home justified before God. For all those who exalt themselves will be humbled, and those who humble themselves will be exalted." (Luke 18:9-14)

Consider this explanation about the flesh and the pride of life from Martin Luther, commenting on "the deceitfulness of sin" mentioned in Hebrews 3:12-13:

This phrase, the deceitfulness of sin, ought to be understood in a much wider sense, so that the term includes even one's own righteousness and wisdom. For more than anything else one's own righteousness and wisdom deceive one and work against faith in Christ, since we love the flesh and the sensations of the flesh and also riches and possessions, but we love nothing more ardently than our own feelings, judgment, purpose, and will, especially when they seem to be good. [7]

Solomon summarized it succinctly when he wrote, "All a person's ways seem pure to them, but motives are weighed by the LORD" (Proverbs 16:2).

Where are you susceptible to letting your own feelings, judgment, purpose, and will deceive you—especially when they seem good?

What the Flesh Looks Like When It Gets Its Way

There's an oft-repeated story that describes our original, sinful nature. It's frequently mis-attributed to the 1926 Minnesota Crime Commission Report, but no matter its authorship, it's thought-provoking:

> Every baby starts life as a little savage. He is completely selfish and self-centered. He wants what he wants when he wants it: his bottle, his mother's atten-tion, his playmate's toys, his uncle's watch, or whatev-er. Deny him these and he seethes with rage and aggressiveness, which would be murderous were he not so helpless.
>
> He's dirty, he has no morals, no knowl-edge, no developed skills. This means

Unless we bring our hearts into alignment with God's plan, the flesh will always gravitate to what is selfish.

that all children, not just certain children, but all children are born delinquent. If permitted to continue in their self-centered world of infancy, given free rein to their impulsive actions to satisfy each want, every child would grow up a criminal, a thief, a killer, a rapist.

Unless we bring our hearts into alignment with God's plan, the flesh will always gravitate to what is selfish.

Here's the best representative list of the acts of the flesh in one location:

The acts of the flesh are obvious: sexual immorality, impurity and debauchery; idolatry and witchcraft; hatred, discord, jealousy, fits of rage, selfish ambition, dissensions, factions and envy; drunkenness, orgies, and the like. I warn you, as I did before, that those who live like this will not inherit the kingdom of God. (Galatians 5:19-21)

What Does the Voice of the Flesh Sound Like in Your Head?

You will hear a once-in-a-while thought from your flesh, such as bitterness about a hurt from the past. But you will also hear recurring thoughts that play to your weaknesses in the form of repetitive temptations. Here are some examples of what the voice of the flesh may sound like.

From the Lust of the Flesh

__ "There's no victim. No one gets hurt."

__ "You deserve to have this pleasure in life."

__ "You won't get caught. No one will ever know."

__ "Don't fight it. It's natural. It's just who you are."

From the Lust of the Eyes

__ "Everyone else is getting theirs. You'd better get yours."

__ "You would be happy if you just had _____."

__ "You *need* that experience/possession."

__ "You can afford it."

From the Pride of Life

__ "You deserved that promotion, not so and so."

__ "They can't tell you what to do."

__ "Are you going to let him get away with disrespecting you like that?"

__ "Why can't they just get their life together like you?"

How does the siren voice of the flesh call out to you? For personal reflection, go back through these sentences and check ones that trigger your flesh on a regular basis.

You can also write other triggers from your flesh here:

_____

_____

_____

_____

_____

Making the Adjustment
Habits and Virtues

These habits and virtues, along with the disciplines in Chapter Two, are concrete tools Christ can use to deliver you from "this body of death" (Romans 7).

1. Prioritize Friendship and a Small Group

During a time when I felt a heavy sense of responsibility, I was mentoring a younger man named Daniel. We met weekly in my home office before work.

One day, we finished about ten minutes early. I said, "Since we have a few extra minutes, can I just tell you a little about what's been going on with me lately?"

He said, "Of course!"

I was able to talk through some of the difficulties I was facing with an autoimmune disease that had lasted, at that point, for three years. I also told him about some health problems in our extended family, and how my wife's mother had just been placed on hospice care the week before.

Before my father-in-law passed away, he appointed my wife as executor of his estate because of my mother-in-law's deteriorating health. Since I have a business background, he asked me to help. Mostly, that meant I sent emails and made copies.

A few days before meeting with Daniel, my wife asked me to print what turned out to be a 20-page document. I grabbed the pages from the printer tray and ran downstairs to put them on her desk.

Halfway there, I noticed the right two inches on every page were cut off during printing, and they were completely useless.

I lost it. I hadn't realized how much pressure had been building inside me, but now it boiled over. I had a meltdown—complete with yelling and cussing.

Thankfully, my wife was not home. But I knew instantly that something was very wrong. I knew the wrong voices had found a way to burglarize my mind.

Even if we do everything humanly possible to burglarproof our minds, those efforts will always be more effective if we're part of a neighborhood watch—guarding what matters to one another as a group.

That's why I wanted to talk to Daniel, and when I shared with him what had taken place, amazingly the cloud lifted. In those brief minutes of being heard by a trusted friend, the frustration that had been accumulating over three years of stressors evaporated. I was able to make the adjustment and take back control of the conversation in my head.

You can do the same thing. Whether it's with one friend or with a small group, trusted confidants who will listen can help you understand what's going on inside your head and make the adjustment. We will always be better together.

One note I want to add: All of us are sinners in need of spiritual friendships to sharpen us. However, even with those friendships, we can hit a wall. If you believe you may be acting out from damaged emotions or the aftermath of abuse or trauma—or maybe you don't *know* why—let me encourage you to work through your story with a good Christian counselor. A counselor helped me significantly at a crucial time.

2. Nurture a Spirit of Humility

In the story of Paul's life, Scripture illustrates a progression toward greater and greater humility. It's also a striking biblical portrait of how we, too, can adjust how we see ourselves over time to become more humble.

Around 55 AD, on his third missionary journey, Paul wrote:

> *For I am **the least of the apostles** and do not even deserve to be called an apostle, because I persecuted the church of God.*
> *(1 Corinthians 15:9, emphasis added)*

Paul already sounds humble, doesn't he? But notice how much he changed over the next seven years. In approximately 62 AD, he wrote while imprisoned in Rome:

> *Although I am **less than the least of all the Lord's people**, this grace was given me: to preach to the Gentiles the boundless riches of Christ."* (Ephesians 3:8, emphasis added)

Notice Paul doesn't think more of himself, but less. But he's not done. Sometime in the mid-60s AD, when he had been set free for a time, he wrote:

> *Here is a trustworthy saying that deserves full acceptance: Christ Jesus came into the world to save **sinners—of whom I am the worst.** (1 Timothy 1:15, emphasis added)*

Here's the progression of how Paul saw himself:

Least of the apostles → Least of the Lord's people → Worst of sinners

How does that work today? My sins are a small fraction of what they were during my early days of following Christ. Discipleship has changed me. I truly am a different person now. That should be an encouragement if you are young in your faith!

However, most of those changes didn't happen overnight, and I'm still growing in two directions. First, each year my understanding of the goodness and greatness of God grows bigger, like the rings on an old tree. But the second direction of my growth has been to see myself in the mirror and realize I'm not as big of a deal as I once thought.

Like Paul, the more we grow in Christ, the more humble we should become.

3. Practice a Lifestyle of Repentance

The foundation of transformation and disciple-making is repentance. It's at the heart of the gospel. Repentance literally means "to change your mind."

Repentance is what the tax collector did when he said, "Lord, have mercy on me, a sinner." The Pharisee did the opposite, continuing in his pride and considering himself better than others.

But repentance is not a once-for-all event at the beginning of salvation. It's part of our lifelong process of sanctification. The very first of the ninety-five theses that Martin Luther nailed to the door of the Wittenberg church says:

> When our Lord and Master Jesus Christ, said "Repent," he intended that the entire life of believers should be repentance.

A lifestyle of repentance requires a commitment to see ourselves as we really are, and then allow the godly sorrow we feel to inspire deep change.

A lifestyle of repentance requires a commitment to see ourselves as we really are, and then allow the godly sorrow we feel to inspire deep change.

For me, repentance works best as a lifestyle of daily—even moment-by-moment—self-awareness.

4. Commit to Personal Discipleship

Mike's wife divorced him after 47 years of marriage. Even though the divorce was completely his fault, he was shattered. Because he didn't have anybody else in his life, Mike decided to become part of a church. The men in the church were ready for him. They took him under their wing. They discipled him.

Three years later, Mike's ex-wife became terminally ill, and he devoted all his time to care for her. After she passed away, his children, from whom he had been alienated, asked him to start attending church with them.

Discipleship changes everything. Discipleship means to know Christ as your Lord by faith, to grow in that faith to become more mature, and then to go serve God through love and good deeds. Discipleship helped Mike master the voices that had turned him into such a toxic man that his wife of 47 years couldn't take it anymore.

Whether you think too highly of yourself or

> *Whether you think too highly of yourself or not highly enough, personal discipleship is God's plan for you to "be transformed by the renewing of your mind."*

not highly enough, personal discipleship is God's plan for you to "be transformed by the renewing of your mind."

Do you need someone to take you under their wing? Is there someone you can take under your wing?

5. Take Personal Responsibility

Concerned about termites, I buried several termite stakes flush with the ground next to the foundation of our home. Each stake had a spring-loaded stem held down by cardboard treated to attract termites. When termites eat the cardboard, a highly visible orange stem pops up.

A couple of months later, five termite stakes popped up. I was discussing the situation with our landscaper, and he said, "Think about it. You installed these termite stakes. They have cardboard treated with something that attracts termites. Why are you surprised? It's like putting bird seed in a bird feeder and then being surprised when birds come to eat it."

In a similar way, we should be careful not to feed our flesh. For example, if you continually experience jealousy or envy because of what people post on social media, change how you consume social media.

It's like putting bird seed in a bird feeder and then being surprised when birds come to eat it.

Personally, after several years of posting spiritual thoughts on Facebook, I saw my brain shift from wanting to be helpful to counting how many likes I was getting. If a post didn't get as many likes as I thought it deserved, I started to let it bother me. Eventually, I realized social media was feeding the voice of the flesh in my mind.

So I took personal responsibility. For me, that meant a six-month Facebook fast that actually ended up lasting three years. I noticed a difference between feeling the need to be heard versus actually having something to say. Now I post occasionally, but no longer to gratify the desires of the flesh with "likes."

6. Create Personal Accountability

John and his wife were traveling and—not for the first time—her directions resulted in John making a wrong turn. John became impatient and said, "You've got to be kidding! Why do you always do that?" Before the dust settled, they both ended up upset and hurt.

A few days later, John called his wife and daughter together and said, "You know, I am an impatient person and I don't want to be that way. I'm sorry. I want to be a better husband and father, and so I'm giving you permission to engage me in this area of my life. I'm asking you to help me be a better husband and father."

He gave them the power to hold him accountable.

About a week later, he asked them how he was doing. They said, "You're doing a lot better, but you still have a way to go. This will take time."

Personal accountability is giving some people permission, like John did, to speak into your life, and then to check in with them about how you're doing.

The flesh gains power through secrecy. Personal accountability helps neutralize that power by bringing a personal weakness or a sinful behavior into the light.

The flesh gains power through secrecy. Personal accountability helps neutralize that power by bringing a personal weakness or a sinful behavior into the light.

Who could you invite to hold you accountable in an area of personal weakness?

7. Practice Selfless Service

One of the most incredible things you can do to neutralize the power of the flesh is to serve others—without expecting anything in return. Jesus said:

> *"So you also, when you have done everything you were told to do, should say, 'We are unworthy servants; we have only done our duty.'" (Luke 17:10)*

I have prayed for one man and his son for a number of years. From time to time, I send him a text to let him know that I'm praying for them, but I never hear back from him. In my flesh, I would like to receive some kind of a response from him—not necessarily a full tit for tat, but it would be nice to hear back from him occasionally.

In the pride of my sinful nature, I'm tempted to retaliate and stop praying. But I find that continuing to pray for that man and his son helps diffuse the power of the flesh in me.

It's hard to embrace the mindset of a servant and have a proud heart at the same time.

A Personal Prayer

Our dearest Father, thank You for giving us the means to work through our sanctification, to neutralize the flesh, and to expose this voice. Thank You for your Scriptures that help us understand how to overcome the lust of the flesh, the lust of the eyes, and the pride of life. We pray that You would help each of us, Lord, to

have someone in our lives who can help us work
through the seven practical habits and virtues
we've just covered. We ask this in Jesus' name.
Amen.

Reflection and Discussion

1. In the space provided, estimate the percentage of your temptations that comes from each of the three dialects of the voice of the flesh. Then, for each one, note something specific that triggers you:

Specific triggers:

- Lust of the flesh: _____%

  _____

- Lust of the eyes: _____%

  _____

- Pride of life: _____%

  _____

2. Why do we keep sinning according to Jeremiah 17:9 and Mark 7:20-23? How does Paul describe his own experience with the sinful nature in Romans 7:15-25?

3. Which of the habits and virtues below are firmly developed in your life (write a check mark next to those) and which ones do you need to strengthen (write an X next to those). Which one can best help you conquer the voice of your flesh, and why?

___ Prioritize Friendship and a Small Group

___ Nurture a Spirit of Humility

___ Practice a Lifestyle of Repentance

___ Commit to Personal Discipleship

___ Take Personal Responsibility

___ Create Personal Accountability

___ Practice Selfless Service

FOUR

The Voice of the Devil

"Simon, Simon, Satan has asked to sift all of you as wheat. But I have prayed for you, Simon, that your faith may not fail. And when you have turned back, strengthen your brothers."

Jesus, Luke 22:31-32

On October 1, 1939, Winston Churchill gave his first wartime radio broadcast to update the British people on the early days of World War II. He said, "I cannot forecast to you the action of Russia. It is a riddle wrapped in a mystery inside an enigma, but perhaps there is a key." [8]

For most people, "a riddle wrapped in a mystery inside an enigma" could easily describe the devil.

Churchill went on to say, "That key is Russian national interest." The key to predicting anyone's behavior, whether friend or foe, is to understand what they want—their interests, needs, goals, purposes, and what they're trying to accomplish. The devil is no different.

So, let's unwrap the mystery of Satan—who he is, what he wants, and how you can readily resist him.

Is the Devil Real?

In some circles, you would be considered unsophisticated and maybe even superstitious to believe the devil is real. But Jesus made statements about Satan that indicate he definitely exists.

Jesus knew the devil as a real being—not a social construct, a figurative person, or a symbolic character, but as a true entity.

In fact, throughout Scripture, no one spoke more about the devil than Jesus. Approximately one-fourth of the 90 or so biblical mentions of Satan or the devil come from Jesus' lips.

During the training of His disciples, Jesus explained that, while the devil was made by God, he is a fallen angel:

> *I saw Satan fall like lightning from heaven. (Luke 10:18)*

Explaining a parable about weeds, Jesus said:

> *The weeds are the people of the evil one, and the enemy who sows them is the devil. (Matthew 13:38-39)*

When Jesus commissioned the apostle Paul, he said:

> *I am sending you to them to open their eyes and turn them from darkness to light, and from the power of Satan to God, so that they may receive forgiveness of sins and a place among those who are sanctified by faith in me. (Acts 26:17-18)*

Jesus knew the devil as a real being—not a social construct, a figurative person, or a symbolic character, but as a true entity.

Who Is the Devil, and What Is He Like?

The Bible is primarily about God, so it doesn't say much about the devil, but what it *does* say gives us a very clear picture of Satan's character and intention. Prominent stories with appearances by Satan include:

- Convincing Adam and Eve in the garden of Eden to disobey God's commands
- Gaining permission from God to afflict Job
- Tempting Jesus in the wilderness
- Entering Judas so he would betray Jesus
- Filling the heart of Ananias so that he lied to the Holy Spirit about money

There's one passage in particular from which we learn quite a lot about the devil. Revelation 12:7-12 says:

*Then war broke out in heaven. Michael and his angels fought against **the dragon**, and **the dragon** and his angels fought back. But he was not strong enough, and they lost their place in heaven.*

The great dragon was hurled down—that ancient serpent called the devil, or Satan, who leads the whole world astray. He was hurled to the earth, and his angels with him.

Then I heard a loud voice in heaven say: "Now have come the salvation and the power and the kingdom of our God, and the authority of his Messiah. For the **accuser** of our brothers and sisters, who accuses them before our God day and night, has been hurled down.

They triumphed over him by the blood of the Lamb and by the word of their testimony; they did not love their lives so much as to shrink from death.

Therefore rejoice, you heavens and you who dwell in them! But woe to the earth and the sea, because **the devil** has gone down to you! He is filled with fury, because **he knows that his time is short.**" (emphasis added)

We'll go deeper into the emphasized parts of this passage in the next section, but for now let me say this: believers need not fear the devil, but it's not wise to ignore him either. With that in mind, let's look at two very different but equally true narratives about the devil.

Narrative 1: The Devil Is a Washed-Up Angel with a Lot of Nicknames

The devil has more nicknames than Muhammad Ali, who never passed up an opportunity to give himself another imaginative label. In the above text alone, Satan is called the dragon, the great dragon, the ancient serpent, the devil, Satan, and the accuser.

Elsewhere, he's referred to as a liar, the father of lies, the evil one, the prince of this world, the ruler of the kingdom of the air, Lucifer, Beelzebub, the serpent, a deceiver, the tempter, and a murderer.

For those without Christ, the devil should be feared, as his nicknames imply. We'll get to that, but this is the part where believers get to make fun of Satan, like Elijah made fun of the false god Baal (see 1 Kings 18:27).

The devil also knows that, if you are in Christ, you have more than enough power to turn him away.

Satan is a washed-up angel with a lot of nicknames. He is like a flea, a gnat, a tick, or a fly that a believer can flick away.

The Scripture from Revelation 12, quoted above, tells us the devil's time is short. He knows it, and he's not happy about it. That's because Satan knows the Scriptures far better than you or I do. He knows that:

> *The reason the Son of God appeared was to destroy the devil's work. (1 John 3:8)*

> *The prince of this world (Satan) now stands condemned. (John 16:11, parenthetic comment added)*

The devil also knows that, if you are in Christ, you have more than enough power to turn him away:

The one who is in you is greater than the one who is in the world. (1 John 4:4)

No temptation has overtaken you except what is common to mankind. And God is faithful; he will not let you be tempted beyond what you can bear. But when you are tempted, he will also provide a way out so that you can endure it. (1 Corinthians 10:13)

What's he left with? The devil is like a cussing parrot sitting on your shoulder, and that's all. As a believer, once you are equipped to turn him away, you can simply tell him, "Shut up. You talk too much."

Still, you need to take the voice of the devil seriously. That's because of the second narrative.

Narrative 2: The Devil Is the CEO of Sin

Satan is the CEO of sin:

"The devil has been sinning from the beginning." (1 John 3:8)

What the devil wants—or, in those words of Churchill, his "national interest"—is to lead the whole world astray (Revelation 12:9). The devil wants to destroy what God wants to build.

Satan is the mass marketer of temptation. The sower of unsolicited sin. The father of fake news. The prince of posers. And he gets a lot of traction by pretending to be one of the good guys:

> *Satan is the mass marketer of temptation. The sower of unsolicited sin. The father of fake news. The prince of posers.*

For Satan himself masquerades as an angel of light. (2 Corinthians 11:14)

And—except for those who receive protection by becoming God's children—for a short[9] while, the devil is getting what he wants:

We know that we are children of God, and that the whole world is under the control of the evil one. (1 John 5:19, emphasis added)

If Satan did not exist, there would be no evil and suffering. His existence is the root cause of every injustice, disease, tragic accident, natural disaster, act of terrorism, racism, oppression, sexual abuse, rape, murder, and act of human trafficking. All temptation, sin, misery, and futility ultimately originate with him.

Even when evil or suffering is not the direct action of the devil, he's still responsible because of what Francis Schaeffer described as "the domino effect of the fall." He set the destruction in motion.

The Limited Power of Satan

That said, Satan is not personally hiding behind every bush. Before we unnecessarily frighten each other over the damage Satan can do, let's make sure we understand his *limitations*.

Satan is not like God. He does not have unlimited power or knowledge, and he can't be everywhere at once. He cannot harm you if you are in Christ:

> *We know that anyone born of God does not continue to sin (habitual sin); the One who was born of God keeps them safe, and the evil one cannot harm them. (1 John 5:18, parenthetic comment added)*

Moreover, Satan does not have the power of death.[10] Scripture clearly tells us that Jesus broke the power of death that held people in bondage:

> *Since the children have flesh and blood, he (Jesus) too shared in their humanity so that by his death he might break the power of him who holds the power of death—that is, the devil—and free those who all their lives were held in slavery by their fear of death. (Hebrews 2:14-15, parenthetical comment added)*

The Bible also tells us that Jesus has authority over Satan.

Then Jesus came to them (his disciples) and said, "All authority in heaven and on earth has been given to me.... And surely I am with you always, to the very end of the age." (Matthew 28:18, 20, parenthetic comment added for clarity)

Perhaps the devil's single biggest accomplishment is to have so successfully exaggerated his power.

Perhaps the devil's single biggest accomplishment is to have so successfully exaggerated his power.

But the truth is, in Christ you are beyond Satan's reach forever. Jesus is always with you. You are not alone.

That's your baseline for when the devil's voice tries to take control of the conversation in your head.

"The Devil Made Me Do It"

The devil can't *make* you do anything. He does not have that kind of power.

Satan did not shove the forbidden fruit down the throats of Adam and Eve. Only you can make yourself sin. No one can force you to say the hurtful words you just spoke. No one can make you lie, cheat, or steal. If you commit adultery, you alone make the choice.

You are responsible for your actions.

What, then, does it mean when someone says, "The devil made me do it"? It means nothing. It's a joke. A way of shifting responsibility.

So, what *can* the devil do?

Satan's only power is deception—he is a deceiver. He can only tempt your lower nature (the flesh) to do the sin your higher nature (the image of God) or your new nature (the new creation) doesn't want to do. Satan can't sin for you—your flesh has to take the bait. He is the tempter, but when we succumb, we are the sinners.[11]

For believers, the power of the devil is limited to temptation. Again:

No temptation has overtaken you except what is common to mankind. And God is faithful; he will not let you be tempted beyond what you can bear. But when you are tempted, he will also provide a way out so that you can endure it. (1 Corinthians 10:13)

Satan is only a voice—a spirit, not a person. He can be as relentless as a stalker ignoring a court order, but he can't get inside your head unless you hold the door open.

Everyone Gets Sifted

The devil can't whisper a word to you without God's permission. For example, in the story of Job, Satan had to appear before God for permission to afflict and test Job's commitment to God.

Likewise, Satan couldn't test any of Jesus' disciples without permission. Jesus said to Peter:

Simon, Simon, Satan has asked to sift all of you as wheat. But I have prayed for you, Simon, that your faith may not fail. And when you have turned back, strengthen your brothers. (Luke 22:31-32)

It's important to see that Satan asked to sift *all* of the disciples, not just Peter. Everyone gets sifted.

> *If you're a believer, Satan fully understands there's no way he can keep you out of heaven.*

And sift them he did! Yet even though all the disciples deserted Jesus on the night He was betrayed, and even though Peter denied three times that he even *knew* Jesus, the Lord did not abandon them.

(Jesus said,) *"I give them eternal life, and they shall never perish; no one will snatch them out of my hand." (John 10:28)*

God has said, "Never will I leave you; never will I forsake you." (Hebrews 13:5)

A bruised reed he will not break, and a smoldering wick he will not snuff out. (Isaiah 42:3)

> The devil's single pleasure is to figure out how to make your life on earth as miserable as possible.

If you're a believer, Satan fully understands there's no way he can keep you out of heaven.

Therefore, the devil's single pleasure is to figure out how to make your life on earth as miserable as possible.

What Does the Voice of the Devil Sound Like in Your Head?

Satan has an arsenal of weapons. He is always probing for a vulnerability.

Of course, the devil loves it when we act on the obvious temptations of the flesh.

But Satan loves nothing more than leveraging the wounded, broken parts of your story. If you've been abused, if your heart was not properly parented, if you struggle to find your identity, if you have suffered trauma, if you battle mental illness, if you've been oppressed, if you're secretly addicted to pornography, if your life lacks meaning and purpose, or wherever else you are experiencing brokenness, then it's a good bet that's where you will hear the devil's voice over and over again.

He delights in distorting healthy human emotions to create excessive feelings of worry, fear, anxiety, anger, hatred, self-loathing, false shame, false guilt, rejection, depression, distrust, doubt, disbelief, and a host of over-compensating reactions.

For example, my first impulse is to see things through the lens of emotional neglect. I have always found it difficult to believe people really care about me personally, and I tend to look for cues that confirm my distrust. I'm loyal to a fault, but once I suspect someone doesn't really care about me, I'm tempted to abruptly cut them off. "If they don't need me, then I don't need them either."

I no longer act on this temptation because I have matured spiritually, but the devil knows this is my biggest lifelong wound that has never fully gone away. So, that's a vulnerability he tries to hack—often in the middle of the night when I can't sleep.

What is the devil's preferred point of attack to get in your head?

Maybe you're vulnerable to the devil's voice in your marriage, work, sense of identity, source of worth, children or grandchildren, friendships, past hurts, finances, faith, sinful behaviors, the relevance of Christianity today, church hurts, or parent wounds.

Wherever you are vulnerable, that's where the devil is most likely to keep inserting those recurring doubts and deceptions. Here are a few examples of what you might hear:

- You don't really think you can be forgiven that easily, do you?
- It's no use. Give up.
- They don't love you. They just love you loving them.
- See? I told you so.
- If God was real, these bad things wouldn't have happened.

- You tried Christianity, but it doesn't work. It's just too hard.
- You can't wait any longer. You need to make something happen.
- You'll never be good enough.

Let's consider the last example. "You'll never be good enough" is actually a completely true statement—but it's not the whole story. We all feel shame and guilt for the bad things we've done. We know we will never be good enough.

But as one of my seminary professors, Dr. Charles "Sherry" McKenzie, liked to say, "It takes a lot of truth to float an error." This is the devil's specialty—to twist the truth just enough to fill your head with doubt.

That's why God, because of His great love for us, made a way to remove this doubt and solve this problem. The gospel is how people who will never be good enough can, nevertheless, still have a close and personal relationship with God.

Resisting the Devil

What does it look like to resist the devil in practice? You know it's him. You know it's a lie. But what can you do to make him flee from you...

- When you wake up in the middle of the night overwhelmed with worry and anxiety about your child making poor choices?
- When you are tempted to despair over how you're going to pay your rent or mortgage?
- When you're tempted to curse God in your grief over a senseless tragedy?
- When you realize the voice in—or trying to get into—your head about your struggling marriage is the devil?

However he tempts you, however deeply the voice of the devil has burrowed into your brain, you can tell the devil to leave:

Resist the devil, and he will flee from you. Come near to God and he will come near to you. (James 4:7-8)

Much of the devil's success can be attributed to how effectively he conceals the ease with which he can be resisted.

Much of the devil's success can be attributed to how effectively he conceals the ease with which he can be resisted.

Yes, Satan has an arsenal of weapons, but God has weapons, too. In the account of Jesus' confrontation with Satan, we see a clear example of how to effectively use those weapons.

How to Recognize and Reject the Devil's Voice

Yes, Satan has an arsenal of weapons, but God has weapons, too.

The best weapon we have is the word of God. We know this because when Jesus interacted directly with Satan, Scripture rendered the devil completely powerless. The story begins like this:

> *Jesus was led by the Spirit into the wilderness to be tempted by the devil. (Matthew 4:1)*

The same Holy Spirit who is in you actually orchestrated Jesus' temptations! Why? To teach us by example how we can reject temptation and sin.

Did Jesus need to be tempted? No, but because he was "tempted in every way, just as we are—yet he did not sin," he understands what you are going through (Hebrews 4:15).

The devil tempted Jesus three different ways.

Temptation 1: Take Matters into Your Own Hands

After fasting forty days and forty nights, he was hungry. The tempter came to him and said, "If you are the Son of God, tell these stones to become bread." (Matthew 4:2-3)

Jesus was hungry. Obviously. Human Jesus would have felt a strong desire for food. But Satan doesn't limit temptations to food; it could be money, sex, or appreciation, for example. Satan can tempt you to take matters into your own hands wherever you have an unmet need or unsatisfied desire.

Satan tried to get Jesus to take matters into His own hands by appealing to pride. "If you're such a big deal, prove it. Show us what you've got."

> *Satan can tempt you to take matters into your own hands wherever you have an unmet need or unsatisfied desire.*

Anyone who has ever watched a college football game with players' tempers flaring knows that a man's pride is often his weak point, and it's the easiest way to get inside an opponent's head.

Jesus shows us the key to recognizing and rejecting the devil's voice when the devil is inciting your pride.

> *Jesus answered, "It is written: 'Man shall not live on bread alone, but on every word that comes from the mouth of God.'" (Matthew 4:4)*

The first principle to defeat the devil's voice is, "We live by the word of God."

Whether it's food, love, sex, money, power, or putting a competitor in his place, when Satan tempts you to take matters into your own hands, first ask, "What does God's word say?"

Temptation 2: Put Yourself in a Position That Requires a Miracle

The second temptation of Jesus took place when the devil took him to stand at the highest point of the temple in the holy city.

> "If you are the Son of God," he said, "throw yourself down. For it is written: 'He will command his angels concerning you, and they will lift you up in their hands, so that you will not strike your foot against a stone.'" (Matthew 4:6)

The devil is very clever. After Jesus appealed to Scripture to defend against him, Satan adapted his second temptation to also appeal to Scripture. One of the easiest ways to deceive someone is to pretend to be of the same party. I hope you understand the devil can out-quote you on Scripture all day long!

Jesus answered him, "It is also written: 'Do not put the Lord your God to the test.'" (Matthew 4:7)

The second principle to defeat the voice of the devil is, "We don't test God."

Suppose you abuse your body—the current temple of the Holy Spirit—with junk food and no exercise, and then you pray for good health. That can easily be compared to jumping off a 10-story temple and expecting God to save you.

When tempted to engage in risky behavior, first ask, "Am I putting myself in a position that will require a miracle by God to get me out of it?"

Temptation 3: Sell Your Soul

The third temptation is caricatured in thousands of books, films, and jokes—selling your soul to the devil in exchange for power, applause, fame, or fortune.

> *Again, the devil took him to a very high mountain and showed him all the kingdoms of the world and their splendor. "All this I will give to you," he said, "if you will bow down and worship me." (Matthew 4:8-9)*

It's doubtful the devil could or would keep this promise, or that it would be worth it if he did. But even if he could, would it really be worth the price of your soul?

The weapon of quoting Scripture enables the well-armed believer to easily reject the voice of this washed-up angel and render him powerless.

When he was a student, author Ken Myers used to buy watery instant coffee out of a machine every day on his way to class. One day, a friend fixed him a cup of freshly brewed coffee. Believe it or not, he didn't like it at first because he was so used to the cheap imitation. Only later did he realize what he had been missing.[12]

Similarly, the world has a lot to offer, but to prefer the world is like drinking instant coffee from a cardboard cup. The cheap imitation is no comparison to the satisfaction that comes from worshipping and serving God.

> *Jesus said to him, "Away from me, Satan! For it is written: 'Worship the Lord your God, and serve him only.'" (Matthew 4:10)*

The third principle to defeat the voice of the devil is to rebuke him directly with: "We worship God and serve Him only."

How do we rebuke the voice of the devil? Jesus set an example for us to follow: Three times Jesus was tempted and three times He quoted Scripture to the devil.

> *Then the devil left him, and angels came and attended him. (Matthew 4:11)*

The weapon of quoting Scripture enables the well-armed believer to easily reject the voice of this washed-up angel and render him powerless.

Making the Adjustment

When it comes to defeating the voice of the devil, all of the tools we have already covered in the "Making the Adjustment" sections in Chapters 2 and 3 can be used to fend off his attacks. But now we come to a special set of tools to conduct spiritual warfare, often referred to as "the full armor of God," as seen in this passage:

Finally, be strong in the Lord and in his mighty power. Put on the full armor of God, so that you can take your stand against the devil's schemes.

For our struggle is not against flesh and blood, but against the rulers, against the authorities, against the powers of this dark world and against the spiritual forces of evil in the heavenly realms.

Therefore put on the full armor of God, so that when the day of evil comes, you may be able to stand your ground, and after you have done everything, to stand. (Ephesians 6:10-13)

The message is clear: You can be strong. You can stand. But what is this full armor of God, and how can you use it to make the devil leave you alone? In Ephesians 6:14-18, Paul goes on to describe six offensive and defensive spiritual weapons:

> Stand firm then, with the belt of truth buckled around your waist, with the breastplate of righteousness in place, and with your feet fitted with the readiness that comes from the gospel of peace. In addition to all this, take up the shield of faith, with which you can extinguish all the flaming arrows of the evil one. Take the helmet of salvation and the sword of the Spirit, which is the word of God. And pray in the Spirit on all occasions with all kinds of prayers and requests. With this in mind, be alert and always keep on praying for all the Lord's people.

Here they are in list form. As you can see, they overlap extensively with the tools we've already explored:

1. *Truth:* Stand firm then, with the belt of truth buckled around your waist.

2. *Righteousness:* with the breastplate of righteousness in place.

3. *The Gospel of Peace:* and with your feet fitted with the readiness that comes from the gospel of peace.

4. *Shield of Faith:* In addition to all this, take up the shield of faith, with which you can extinguish all the flaming arrows of the evil one.

5. *The Word of God:* Take the helmet of salvation and the sword of the Spirit, which is the word of God.

6. *Prayer:* And pray in the Spirit on all occasions with all kinds of prayers and requests. With this in mind, be alert and always keep on praying for all the Lord's people.

They are both simple and complex. You can use them immediately, and you can spend the rest of your life learning how to use them better.

For centuries, the most popular way to put on your armor is during daily devotions. A daily quiet time builds on all of the spiritual disciplines, habits, and virtues we've discussed, but especially prayer and God's word. Then, when under attack, the truth of God will make your heart and mind strong.

A Sentence to Control the Devil

Now I want to give you the single most practical weapon I have found to kick the voice of the devil out of my head—or resist him from getting in there in the first place.

It's a sentence I've repeated thousands of times that, as I recall, I first heard from evangelist Billy Graham.

It's a sentence synthesized from Scripture. In all three of His temptations, Jesus points us to the word of God: "It is written." But in the last response, Jesus adds a verbal rebuke: "Away from me, Satan!"

Elsewhere we read:

- In Zechariah 3:2, God said, "The LORD rebuke you, Satan!"

- In Jude 1:9, the archangel Michael said, "The Lord rebuke you!"

- In Matthew 16:23, when Jesus saw the devil was using Peter as a stumbling block, He said, "Get behind me, Satan!"

Every time I repeat this sentence—often several times a day—I feel whatever cloud of emotional oppression or sinful temptation bothering me immediately go away.

Sometimes I say it out loud, but usually as part of the mental conversation to control what's going on inside my head. The sentence is:

"Satan, I rebuke you
in the name of the Lord Jesus Christ."

There is no magic in the exact wording. Martin Luther, who struggled mightily against Satan, reportedly once picked up his inkwell and hurled it across the room, saying, "I am baptized! I am baptized!" That was Luther's version of, "Satan, I rebuke you in the name of the Lord Jesus Christ." (An inkwell...*really?* When he saw the mess, I'm sure he wished he had thrown a book instead!)

You can memorize this sentence exactly or make a version of your own, as Luther did. Whichever words you choose, you can

> "Satan, I rebuke you in the name of the Lord Jesus Christ."

silence the voice of the devil by invoking the authority of Jesus Christ.

A Personal Prayer

Our dearest Father, thank You that while there's not a lot about the devil in Scripture, what You have given us is more than enough to understand that he is extremely limited in power. His time is short. Greater is He who is in us than he who is in the world. And by the blood of the Lamb and the word of our testimony, we can drive out the devil's voice. We can say, "Satan, I rebuke you in the name of the Lord Jesus Christ." Grant us confidence that the devil has no power over us that we cannot thwart with the simple name of Jesus Christ, in whose name we now pray. Amen.

Reflection and Discussion

1. Refer back to the section "What Does the Voice of the Devil Sound Like in Your Head?" on page 116. What is the area where you are most vulnerable to the devil's arsenal of weapons, and why?

2. Fill in the blanks for the six elements of the armor God has given us to resist and reject "the devil's schemes" in Ephesians 6:14-18.

   1. Belt of T_____
   2. Breastplate of R_____
   3. Feet Fitted with Readiness of the Gospel of P_____
   4. Shield of F_____
   5. Helmet of Salvation and Sword of the Spirit, which is the W_____ of God
   6. P_____ in the Spirit

Next, put a check mark by the armor you feel skilled at using, and explain why. Where do you need more training, and why?

3. Recall a situation when the sentence, "Satan, I rebuke you in the name of the Lord Jesus Christ," would have helped you resist the voice of the devil. Why not write this sentence on a post-it and stick it to your mirror? Or set it up as a daily reminder on your phone until it becomes second nature when you hear the devil's voice tempting you?

FIVE

The Voice of the Holy Spirit

*What we have received is not the spirit
of the world, but the Spirit who is from
God, so that we may understand
what God has freely given us.*

1 Corinthians 2:12

Our marriage got off to a clumsy start. The little I knew about manhood, marriage, and parenting had been pieced together from a collection of stereotypes and clichés. Within a few months of our wedding, I was desperate for help.

So one Sunday morning, we found our way to a local church, walked up the sidewalk, and opened the door. And when we walked in, the people there were ready for both of us, but especially me—an inexperienced husband looking for help and hope.

One week later, Dan Stanley and his wife, Meta, invited us to visit a class they were teaching for young married couples. Flattered to be asked, we said yes.

Because I was very much caught up in the world, I thought the class would be a good place to meet some potential investors for my real estate deals. So, I put on the expensive suit I had purchased to impress people, and off we went.

About 20 of us sat in a circle on those uncomfortable chocolate milk colored metal chairs found in every other church on the planet. I slouched in my chair, legs stretched out, hands in my pockets, staring at the terrazzo floor and daydreaming about my upcoming work week.

I was jolted back to the present moment when Dan read from his Bible:

> *Husbands, love your wives, just as Christ loved the church and gave himself up for her. (Ephesians 5:25)*

A lightning bolt of heat flashed through my body. My clothing was immediately soaked with an inexplicable amount of perspiration. My face flushed beet red. I've never been so embarrassed. Complete humiliation. I couldn't look up. My eyes riveted on the terrazzo. I just knew every pair of eyeballs in that circle was focused on me, filled with disdain and derision.

Had Dan been talking to my wife behind my back? I had no idea how he had discovered the truth, but I knew I had been found out. I was a fraud, and now everyone knew what a terrible husband I had been.

As it turned out, he kept speaking. When I could finally lift my head, I saw no one looking at me. They had all moved on. Whatever happened was entirely between God and me.

Later, I learned there's a name for what happened: conviction of sin. True conviction is the Holy Spirit convincing a person that he or she has fallen short of what God intended. It isn't to bring lasting shame and grief, but rather a godly sorrow that leads us to repent.

The first time I heard the Spirit's voice, however, I didn't even know He existed! But in spite of that, He was still working—working to reveal my need for help, to get me to that church, and to usher me into that class.

> *True conviction is the Holy Spirit convincing a person that he or she has fallen short of what God intended.*

The goals for this chapter are for you to easily recognize the Holy Spirit's voice and to be so filled with His power and presence that there's as little room as possible for the competing voices.

But first, who is the Holy Spirit, where does He come from, and what does He do?

Who Is the Holy Spirit?

The Bible calls the Holy Spirit our Paraclete (from the Greek word *parakletos*). Literally, this means "one who helps." He is God *with us* and has many roles.

According to Scripture, He is our helper, comforter, counselor, guide, and advocate. He convicts and converts. He intercedes for us with groans so deep that words cannot express. He bestows on each of us different spiritual gifts. He empowers us to be His witnesses, make disciples, pursue the spiritual disciplines, love one another, do good deeds, put on Christian virtues, and enjoy the fruit that grows when we understand how to walk in His presence and power.

What is that fruit?

The fruit of the Spirit is love, joy, peace, forbearance, kindness, goodness, faithfulness, gentleness and self-control. (Galatians 5:22-23)

Not surprisingly, much of what we know about the Holy Spirit we learn from Jesus:

"If you love me, keep my commands. And I will ask the Father, and he will give you another advocate to help you and be with you forever—the Spirit of truth." (John 14:15-17a)

> *"But very truly I tell you, it is for your good that I am going away. Unless I go away, the Advocate will not come to you; but if I go, I will send him to you." (John 16:7)*

> *"The world cannot accept him, because it neither sees him nor knows him. But you know him, for he lives with you and will be in you. I will not leave you as orphans; I will come to you." (John 14:17b-18)*

The Father and Jesus give us the Spirit, who is fully God. Be sure to see in these verses that the third person of the Trinity is a "Him," not an "It."

Importantly, the voice of the Spirit does not speak on His own, but He communicates only what the Father and Jesus tell Him.

> *But when he, the Spirit of truth, comes, he will guide you into all the truth. He will not speak on his own; he will speak only what he hears, and he will tell you what is yet to come. (John 16:13)*

> *"But the Advocate, the Holy Spirit,*
> *whom the Father will send in my name,*
> *will teach you all things and will remind*
> *you of everything I have said to you."*
> *(John 14:26)* [13]

The Holy Spirit is appointed as our Guardian so that He can watch over us with His power, protection, provision, tutelage, and loving care.

When the Spirit speaks to us, how can we know it's Him?

What Does the Voice of the Holy Spirit Sound Like in Your Head?

We live on a lake. We often see osprey and occasionally eagles. One day, an osprey flew by, and I wondered, *Is that an eagle?*

No, it was an osprey.

Another day, I was looking out the window and saw a large bird. *Is that an eagle?*

No, it was an osprey.

Then one day, I looked out the window, and I said, "Oh, my gosh, it's an eagle!"

When you see an eagle, you don't have to ask, "Is that an eagle?" It's obvious. And when you hear the Spirit, you don't need to ask, "Is that the Holy Spirit?" You'll know.

When you hear the Spirit, you don't need to ask, "Is that the Holy Spirit?" You'll know.

The Spirit will never say anything that contradicts what the Father and Jesus have already said in Scripture. The contents of the message will remain consistent; yet the ways the Spirit speaks vary widely. Here are some examples:

- Your pulse quickens, your heart throbs, and you let out a deep sigh as you read a verse of Scripture. In that moment, you sense His holy presence because "the Spirit himself testifies with our spirit that we are God's children" (Romans 8:16).
- You feel like the pastor is speaking directly to you.
- While reading a Christian book you laugh to yourself, "I think this author has been reading my mail!"

- The earnest words of a faithful friend carry the distinct ring of truth.
- You need wisdom on what to do next, and a Bible verse comes to mind.
- You pray and have a calm assurance that God has heard you.

One day, I was smarting from being criticized by a man I had to lay off during a painful business downturn. Things were already tough and I felt

The Spirit will never say anything that contradicts what the Father and Jesus have already said in Scripture.

overwhelmed with disappointment. His harshness toward me was the last straw. I felt a wave of bitterness sweep over me. I prayed, "God, on top of everything else I'm going through right now, please don't let me also become a bitter person."

I heard an inaudible but distinct voice in my head: "Praise me." That was all the Spirit said. At that point in my spiritual journey, I had no idea what that meant. So, I turned on some worship songs, cranked up the volume until my car windows rattled, and turned my thoughts toward the goodness and greatness of God. The bitterness disappeared that day and never returned.

Sometimes, the voice of the Spirit will thunder in your head, like in the conviction of sin I experienced at the marriage class. Other times, He will guide you with a quiet affirmation that you are on the right path—or a clear discomfort that you're on the wrong path. You may feel a wave of godly sorrow wash over you that leads you to repentance.

Sometimes, the Spirit will fill you to the bursting point with an overwhelming sense of how much He loves and accepts you. Other times, He will fill you with that same kind of love and acceptance for someone who is struggling like a bird with a broken wing.

Some days, you will find yourself in someone else's storm, and you'll realize the Spirit put you there so He would have an insider positioned to speak words of comfort, truth, and love.

Other days, like prophets of old, you may find a fierce, holy indignation boiling inside you over all the evil in the world. The Spirit may compel you to act. Or, He may block you from taking an action you were sure was good and right—only for you to be grateful later.

Where once you were afraid, tremendous courage may surge in the face of adversity. Or the Spirit will deeply encourage you, even as you endure great sorrow. Other times, He may warn you of hardships to come.

You may tremble with an overwhelming awareness of His holiness—driven to your knees, or even to lie face down in His presence. And sometimes you will feel such exultation that you ask God to stay His hand as your spirit soars within you. You delight in Him, and you feel His delight with you.

> *God may speak to you in dramatic displays of power, but the whisper of God can be just as overwhelming.*

God may speak to you in dramatic displays of power, but the whisper of God can be just as overwhelming, as illustrated in this encounter the prophet Elijah had with God:

> *The LORD said, "Go out and stand on the mountain in the presence of the LORD, for the LORD is about to pass by."*
>
> *Then a great and powerful wind tore the mountains apart and shattered the rocks before the LORD, but the LORD was not in the wind.*
>
> *After the wind there was an earthquake, but the LORD was not in the earthquake.*
>
> *After the earthquake came a fire, but the LORD was not in the fire. And after the fire came a gentle whisper.*
>
> *When Elijah heard it, he pulled his cloak over his face and went out and stood at the mouth of the cave. Then a voice said to him, "What are you doing here, Elijah?" (1 Kings 19:11-13)*

Every time you feel the urge to worship, yearn for deeper communion with God, desire to put on Christian virtues, resolve to practice spiritual disciplines, commit to do your work as if working for the Lord, pledge to make disciples, or feel spurred on to exercise your spiritual gifts in selfless acts of love and good deeds, you can have full confidence that the Holy Spirit's voice is stirring your heart and mind.

You don't need to be a mystic, a prophet, or a theologian. Hearing the Holy Spirit is part of the normal Christian experience.

As our premise says, however, those three other voices are also part of our normal experience, like barking dogs. The Spirit is the one voice who can help you put a muzzle on the world, the flesh, and the devil.

> *Hearing the Holy Spirit is part of the normal Christian experience.*

How can you be so filled with the Spirit's presence and power that you leave as little room as possible for the other voices?

Experiencing His Presence and Power

I grew up with motorcycles. But when I brought home my first Harley, I ran into a problem. The next day I was up before dawn for my first ride, but it wouldn't start. I checked the gas and jiggled the ignition. I tried everything I could think of—even removed and replaced the battery cables. Nothing. The most powerful motorcycle I had ever owned had become a 650-pound paperweight.

My irritation reached the boiling point. I called the dealership and said, "This stupid motorcycle won't start. There's something defective with this thing. I want you to come and take it back because I don't want it anymore."

The calm service rep asked me a few questions. "Did you turn on the ignition?"

"Well, of course I turned on the ignition."

"Okay, did you check the gas?"

"Yes, I checked the gas."

"Did you make sure the fuel cock was open?"

"Yes, I made sure the fuel cock was open."

"Did you make sure the battery cables are properly secured?"

"Yes, I made sure the battery cables are secure."

"Did you check the on/off switch on the handlebars?"

I said, "What are you talking about, the on/off switch on the handlebars?"

I'm sure you have wondered why so many professing Christians don't live powerful, transformed lives. Here's your answer: Like my experience of not knowing how to turn on my powerful motorcycle, they don't know how to turn on the Spirit's powerful voice. Let's look at how the Spirit works—and then what you can do to turn on the power.

The Spirit speaks to each of us in different ways at different times through:

- the baptism of the Spirit,
- being filled with the Spirit, and
- walking by the Spirit.

The Baptism of the Spirit

At conversion, when we put our faith in Jesus Christ, we are simultaneously baptized with the Holy Spirit. Our bodies literally become the temples in which He lives. The apostle Paul explained this in the following passages:

> *For we were all baptized by one Spirit so as to form one body—whether Jews or Gentiles, slave or free —and we were all given the one Spirit to drink. (1 Corinthians 12:13)*

> *Do you not know that your bodies are temples of the Holy Spirit, who is in you, whom you have received from God? (1 Corinthians 6:19)*

Nevertheless, many believers still find themselves living weak and tepid lives.

That's because while every believer is *baptized* with the Holy Spirit, not every believer is being *filled* with the Spirit.

Being Filled with the Spirit

While the baptism of the Holy Spirit is a once-in-a-lifetime experience, to be filled with the Holy Spirit is an ongoing, continuous process of regularly "topping off" in your relationship with God.

Being filled with the Spirit provides constant, unlimited access to God's presence and power all day every day:

> *Do not get drunk on wine, which leads to debauchery. Instead, be filled with the Spirit. (Ephesians 5:18)*

It's just common sense. Every source of power needs to be replenished regularly, whether that's food and water for your body, gas for your car, propane for your furnace, or the Spirit for your soul.

> *Every source of power needs to be replenished regularly, whether that's food and water for your body, gas for your car, propane for your furnace, or the Spirit for your soul.*

To be filled is something God does for you, but you also have the privilege of cooperating. In the "Making the Adjustment" section at the end of this chapter, we'll look at how you can be baptized and filled with the Spirit.

But before we go there, what happens when you *are* filled with the Spirit?

Walking by the Spirit

The purpose of baptism and filling is to empower you to walk in the power of the Spirit.

The best recipes are the simplest. The more ingredients you add, the more complicated it becomes—and the more difficult to get right.

God has kept His recipe for transformation simple:

> *So I say, walk by the Spirit, and you will not gratify the desires of the flesh. (Galatians 5:16)*

To "walk by the Spirit" is to activate the power of God:

> *But you will receive power when the Holy Spirit comes on you. (Acts 1:8)*

The Greek word for "power" is *dunamis*, from which we get "dynamite." The voice of the Spirit carries explosive power. When I finally did figure out how to crank up my motorcycle, the explosion of gasoline in the cylinders transformed my paperweight into a powerful beast.

The same kind of explosive power will transform you as you increasingly learn how to discern the Spirit's voice and depend on His presence and power.

Hudson Taylor, the pioneer missionary to China, said:

> Many Christians estimate difficulties in the light of their own resources, and thus attempt little and often fail at the little they attempt. All God's giants have been weak men who did great things for God because they reckoned on His power and presence with them. [14]

How about you? Are you making a difference for God? Understanding how to walk in the presence and power of the Holy Spirit is the meat of the coconut when it comes to loving and serving God with your whole heart.

Read on and let me show you how you can turn on the power of the Spirit's voice.

Making the Adjustment
Habits and Virtues

How to Experience the Baptism of the Spirit

1. Surrender to Jesus Christ

The single most powerful thing you can do to silence the barking of the world, flesh, and devil is to receive Jesus Christ as your Savior and Lord.

Conversion is the work of the Holy Spirit:

> *He saved us through the washing of rebirth and renewal by the Holy Spirit, whom he poured out on us generously through Jesus Christ our Savior, so that, having been justified by his grace, we might become heirs having the hope of eternal life. (Titus 3:5-7)*

Have you settled the issue of your salvation? If not, are you ready to respond to the voice of the Spirit drawing you to faith in Jesus? I invite you to make your move. You can ask for His grace by using this model prayer:

Lord Jesus, I need You. Your Holy Spirit is drawing me to believe in You. The Holy Spirit's voice is in my head. By faith, I humbly ask You to be my Savior and Lord. I confess that I have lived a sinful life, and I want to change. Transform me into the person You created me to be. In Your name I pray. Amen.

If you have just given your life to Christ, welcome to the family! For your next three steps: tell someone what you've done, start reading the Bible for yourself, and find an experienced Christian or small group to take you under their wing and show you the ropes.

> *The single most powerful thing you can do to silence the barking of the world, flesh, and devil is to receive Jesus Christ as your Savior and Lord.*

Learn more about spiritual mentoring and download a free digital Coaching Guide at maninthemirror.org/the-christian-man, which you can discuss with a more mature Christian.

Now that you have declared or affirmed your faith in Jesus, let's look at how you can be filled with the Spirit.

How to Be Continuously Filled with the Holy Spirit

Ephesians 5:18-20 includes two concrete habits that we can add to our growing list of "making the adjustment" ideas.

2. Actively Engage in a Local Church

Crucially, you can't be filled or stay filled in isolation.

> *Instead, be filled with the Spirit, speaking to one another with psalms, hymns, and songs from the Spirit. Sing and make music from your heart to the Lord. (Ephesians 5:18-19)*

> *And let us consider how we may spur one another on toward love and good deeds. (Hebrews 10:24)*

I like the story of a man who actively participated in a church for several years but suddenly stopped attending. His pastor dropped by one evening unannounced. The man answered the door and invited him in. Of course, he knew why his pastor was there.

They went and sat on two chairs in front of a roaring fire. Neither man said anything. After a few minutes, the pastor picked up the fire tongs, took one of the logs out of the fire, and laid it on the hearth.

The flames died down and flickered a few times before going out. They watched in silence as the log started to grow cold.

After a while, the pastor once again picked up the fire tongs and put the smoldering wood back with the burning logs. It immediately burst back into flame.

The pastor got up and said, "Well, I need to go now. But I've enjoyed our visit."

The man rose too and said, "I appreciate your message, pastor. I will be in church on Sunday."

We really do grow cold in our faith when we try to walk with God alone.

Every predator understands the strategic value of isolation. The devil knows that if he can separate you from the voices of your support community, he can surround you with the sounds of the world and the flesh.

God puts us in communities of faith for our protection. There is strength in numbers.

3. Cultivate an Attitude of Gratitude

The Ephesians passage concludes:

"Always giving thanks to God our Father for everything, in the name of our Lord Jesus Christ." (Ephesians 5:20)

Nothing will drain your tank faster than an ungrateful attitude.

Robert saw quite a bit of potential in Tim and invited him to an important meeting. Throughout the day, Tim made incredible contributions. You could see his star rising.

But not once during the meeting did Tim even acknowledge Robert's presence. When the six-hour meeting was over—it went through lunch—the group dismissed. Everybody was congratulating Tim for the part he played in the meeting. Even after the meeting, Tim never expressed gratitude to Robert for recognizing his potential and giving him the opportunity.

We can easily see Tim's foolishness, but now let's apply that to our relationship with God. He sees a lot of potential in you. You could say He invites you to the meeting. To be filled with the Holy Spirit includes having a spirit of gratitude for all God is doing for you.

Psalm 118:22-24 (ESV) entreats:

> *The stone that the builders rejected has become the cornerstone. This is the LORD's doing; it is marvelous in our eyes. This is the day the LORD has made; let us rejoice and be glad in it.*

For years I wondered, *How is that even possible? I'm having a horrendous day.* But then I learned the Hebrew word for "rejoice" can be a *feeling* or an *attitude.*

Let me ask you. Can you think of anything that makes you happier than when a child says, "Thank you"—especially if you've made a sacrifice for them? Or, for that matter, is anything more deflating than you making a big sacrifice, and then having a child take it for granted?

God sacrificed His own Son so that we could have eternal life. So even on those days when we don't *feel* grateful, we can still—because of our faith—have an attitude of gratitude.

How to Walk by the Spirit

4. Do Your Part by Faith

Walking by the Spirit consists of *God's* part and *our* part:

> *Therefore, my dear friends, as you have always obeyed—not only in my presence, but now much more in my absence—continue to work out your salvation with fear and trembling, for it is God who works in you to will and to act in order to fulfill his good purpose. (Philippians 2:12-13)*

God's part is to give us the desire ("to will") and power ("to act") to do His will. Our part is to continue to work out our salvation in humble, obedient reverence and awe.

Bill Bright, founder of Cru (Campus Crusade for Christ International), wrote in "Have You Made the Wonderful Discovery of the Spirit-Filled Life?"[15] that faith is the only means by which a Christian can live the Spirit-directed life.

That is 100 percent true. If you have faith, nothing else matters. And if you don't have faith, nothing else matters.

To have faith simply means to believe you're saved by grace, without regard to how many good things you may or may not do.

> If you have faith, nothing else matters. And if you don't have faith, nothing else matters.

When I first trusted in Jesus, I believed I was saved by faith, but I thought it was up to me to prove that God hadn't made a mistake. Essentially, I believed I was saved by faith, but needed to *add* something to keep it.

But that's not Christianity! Nothing you do will ever make you good enough to deserve salvation and, likewise, nothing you ever do or don't do will make you unworthy to keep it.

It's equally true, however, that not much is going to happen in your life unless you put in some effort. It's like the story of a man who drove his family into the country and came upon a beautiful, lush farm with neatly manicured rows of grain. The farmer happened to be getting his mail, so the man stopped to say hello. "God sure has blessed you with a beautiful farm," he said.

"Yes, He has," the farmer replied. "Of course, you should have seen this place when He had it all to Himself!"

I remember one day in seminary when theologian R. C. Sproul wrote this on the whiteboard:

WRONG: Faith + Works = Salvation

WRONG: Faith = Salvation

RIGHT: Faith = Salvation + Works

Doing our part adds nothing to our salvation, because it's based on faith, not works. That said, investing some effort is a sign of faith.

That's why the chapters of this book conclude with spiritual disciplines, habits, and virtues. They are tools

> *Investing some effort is a sign of faith.*

that can help you do your part to take control of the conversation in your head.

5. Regularly Renew Your Faith

Another part of the normal Christian experience is to feel like you've lost your *dunamis*—the power of God. What can you do when you realize you are no longer walking in the presence and power of the Spirit?

> *If we confess our sins, he is faithful and just and will forgive us our sins and purify us from all unrighteousness. (1 John 1:9)*

Any time you sin by listening to the wrong voices, confess them, and ask the Holy Spirit to once again fill you with His power. You can pray like this:

You can and should pray this or a similar prayer anytime you are not in right relationship with God for any reason.

Lord Jesus, I need You in my life right now more than I ever have. I do believe, but I confess I have gotten off track. I have not allowed the presence and power of Your Spirit to direct and guide my life as I should. I have sinned, and I am sorry. By faith, I ask You to forgive me once again and restore me to a right relationship with You. Fill me with Your Spirit and change me into the person You want me to become. In Your name I pray. Amen.

You can and should pray this or a similar prayer anytime you are not in right relationship with God for any reason. Confessing your sins as they happen is a key feature of the Spirit-filled life.

6. Ask for Help

There's a story about a little boy helping his father with yard work. His father asked him to clear rocks in a certain area of the yard. After a while, the boy was straining to pull up a huge rock buried in the dirt. The little boy struggled and struggled while his father watched.

Finally, the boy gave up and said, "I can't do it."

His father asked, "Did you use all of your strength?"

The little boy looked hurt and said, "Yes, sir. I used every ounce of strength I have."

His father said, "No, you didn't. You didn't ask me to help."

Then the father walked over and the two of them easily pulled that big rock out of the dirt.

When the world's worries, values, and philosophies reel you in, it is the Holy Spirit whose voice is always there to guide you—and more so if you ask for help.

When the carnal or selfish desires of the flesh are tempting you, it is the Holy Spirit whose voice will provide a way of escape—and more so if you ask for help.

When the devil attacks your frailties or weak points, it is the Holy Spirit whose voice will give you the power and the words to make him flee—and more so if you ask for help.

The Holy Spirit is our helper. Asking for help, like putting forth effort, is another evidence of faith. Let Him help you.

And when you fail, as we all do, it is the Holy Spirit whose voice will prompt you to turn back and confess your sins. He will forgive you and restore you to a right relationship with Jesus and the Father—and more so if you ask for help.

The Holy Spirit is our helper. Asking for help, like putting forth effort, is another evidence of faith. Let Him help you.

A Personal Prayer

Our dearest Father, thank You for Your Holy Spirit. Spirit, we ask You to wash and renew us in the gospel of Jesus Christ. Fill us with Your presence and power. Teach us all things and remind us of everything He said so that we may walk by the Spirit. Give us ears to hear Your voice, wisdom to apply it, and courage to share this good news with every willing person. We make our prayer in the name of Jesus. Amen.

The final chapter is a harmony of what I believe the Holy Spirit wants you to take away. But first, please complete the questions.

Reflection and Discussion

1. Describe an experience when you believe you heard the voice of the Holy Spirit. Why did you think it was the Spirit?

2. What are the differences between the baptism of the Spirit, being filled with the Spirit, and walking by the Spirit? Why is investing effort a sign of faith?

3. Which of the following did you most need to hear or be reminded of, and why?

1.   Surrender to Jesus Christ
2.   Engage in a Local Church
3.   Cultivate an Attitude of Gratitude
4.   Participate Through Faith
5.   Regularly Renew Your Faith
6.   Ask for Help

SIX

A Message to You
from the Holy Spirit

While writing this book, I felt a deep desire—almost a burden—to convey to you how much God loves you, personally. With that on my mind, I decided to take a step back from writing one day and went hiking. As I walked through the woods, surrounded by the beauty of His creation, Scripture started flooding my mind and became this chapter. Every word is based on Scripture, and I believe this is what the voice of the Holy Spirit wants you to hear.

_____, (insert your name here)

Jesus is one with the Father, I am one with them, and together we are God. Let me speak to you on our behalf.

I love you very much, and I only want what's best for you. I will never forsake you or leave you alone.

Every day, I long to be in a close relationship with you. I want you to start each day with me. I want to talk to you, and I want you to talk to me.

Tell me your sorrows. Show me where it hurts. Ask for help. Are you happy? Are you experiencing joy? Share that with me, too.

> *I want you to start each day with me.*

During those times when you don't like your lot in life very much, turn to me. Trust me with all your hurts, bruises, and wounds—both the ones you can describe and the ones beyond your understanding. I will heal them.

When you hear my voice, do not harden your heart. My sheep listen to my voice, and I shepherd them.

Abide in me, and I will fill you with my love, joy, peace, patience, kindness, goodness, faithfulness, gentleness, and self-control.

Worship me in the beauty of my holiness, the majesty of my creation, the unconditional nature of my love, the generosity of my salvation, and the mystery of my providence.

Everything I do is good, and all my ways are just. I will never tell you to do anything that contradicts what I have said through the Scriptures I preserved for you.

I will never tell you to do anything that contradicts what I have said through the Scriptures I preserved for you.

I have plans for all my children—plans beyond your comprehension. You must always remember your life in the larger perspective of my plan and purpose for all people, the world, and eternity. I am working out everything to conform with the purpose of my will.

This is my will—that you love me and obey my word. My commands are not burdensome, but for your good.

Love one another and be kind. Always remember that people are fragile. Freely forgive. Be just. Love mercy. Serve others. Take care of the poor. Don't be selfish. Look out not only for your own interests, but also for the interests of others. In everything, give thanks.

> This is my will—
> that you love
> me and obey
> my word.

Seek and save those who are lost. I will empower you to disciple them to love, follow, and serve me. You need people, and they need you. I love you. I love them. I am love. I am truth.

My Scriptures provide a refuge and a double-edged sword. They say exactly what I want to say, exactly the way I want to say it. Every word of my voice will accomplish what I desire and achieve the purpose for which I sent it.

I know what you need before you ask, and I love to hear you pray. I will always answer your prayers, and I will always give you whatever you ask for according to the will of my larger plan and purpose. Even when your prayers cannot be answered exactly the way you hope, you have my promise that I will never give you less than as much as you need.

You have my promise that I will never give you less than as much as you need.

Today is a day I made for you. Rejoice and be glad in it. Some days, you will be able to rejoice because you feel it in your bones. Other days, you can still rejoice, because I am good. You can trust me.

When you are bruised, I will heal you. When your faith is weak, I will revive you. The foundation of our relationship is your faith in Jesus.

If you draw near to me, you'll find that I am very near. I will protect you from the voices of the world, the flesh, and the devil. The whole world is under the control of the evil one, but he cannot harm you, for I will keep you safe and make you wise.

Guard your heart and fear no evil. Other people are not your enemy. They are not the villain. It's the sin in them that is the villain. I have overcome sin.

I have allowed many wrongs to happen in the world. You will be tested, stretched, and even hated, but you can trust me. At just the right time, I will lift you up, both in this life and the next.

Settle in the places I have appointed for you to live. If your circumstances are not good, and you can improve them, I want you to improve them. If you cannot, I want you to know that I am with you always, and you will always be with me. I am always interceding for you with groans so deep that words cannot express them.

> I am always interceding for you with groans so deep that words cannot express them.

Whether your circumstances are easy or difficult, always remember that life is a breath—a vapor that appears for a little while and then vanishes, only to reappear before the throne of my glory in heaven. Let my holiness wash over you. Humble yourself before my greatness and goodness.

Life is a beautiful idea. When I looked at all I had created, I imagined what it would be like for you to inhabit my creation, and that brought my heart great joy.

When I looked at all I had created, I imagined what it would be like for you to inhabit my creation, and that brought my heart great joy.

That's why I created you. That's why you are here, and that's why you will one day be with me for eternity. You are fearfully and wonderfully made. So rejoice and be glad!

Are you anxious? Cast all your anxiety on me, because I care for you.

Are you worried? Don't be. I have your name written on the palm of my hand, and I will take care of you.

Are you distressed? Whatever is troubling your heart troubles my heart too, and I will take care of it in due time. I have an altogether different way of looking at time that you cannot understand. But I haven't forgotten you for a moment.

When you go through great trials, do not be afraid. Imagine yourself in my arms, because you are.

I am the God who is, who was, and is to come. Listen to my voice.

Reflection and Discussion

1. For this final reflection and discussion, share how the Holy Spirit has spoken to you while reading, reflecting on, and discussing this book.

2. Now that you have a better handle on how to distinguish between the four voices, describe a recent situation in which you've felt confused or overwhelmed. Is the main source of those feelings the voice of world, the flesh, the devil, or the Holy Spirit? Explain your answer.

3. Using Appendix 1, review the tools and skills from the Making the Adjustment sections of this book. Which ones will most help you going forward, and why?

AFTERWORD

Thank you for letting me be part of your life for a few hours. It's a profound privilege that I don't take lightly. As you finish this book and move on to other things, I hope you will:

- Regularly ask, "Is that thought the voice of the world, the flesh, the devil, or the Holy Spirit?"
- Devote yourself to pursuing the tools and skills that will guard your heart and equip you to make any needed adjustments.
- Share this book with someone you love.

I pray God will give you control over every thought that tries to complicate your life and drag you down. May you always walk in the power and presence of the Spirit's voice.

Acknowledgements

Rarely has one person owed so much to so many.

I'm deeply indebted to Shane Flannery, Rick Fletcher, Dave Kopp, Patsy Morley, and John Vonberg for serving as critical readers of the manuscript. Dozens of their suggestions transformed this book into something far more readable.

Jamie Turco and Ruth Ford deserve special credit for editing the book. I don't know what I would do without their ingenious insights. It certainly would not have been a book you would have wanted to read!

Carolyn Bennett Fraiser receives my double gratitude for both proofreading and designing the exceptional layout for the printers. Jeremy Kennedy came up with the captivating cover design. And special appreciation goes to Pat Leupold who was a meticulous second proofreader.

I'm grateful to the men of The Man in the Mirror Bible Study for letting me use them as guinea pigs as I worked out how to present this material to you, my reader.

Finally, everyone on the Man in the Mirror team has made this book possible, but I especially want to thank those who published the book itself: Brett Clemmer, Dale Redder, and Bryan Richardson.

APPENDIX 1

Making the Adjustment
Summary Chart

Chapter 2: Spiritual Disciplines
to Hear from God

1. The Bible: What Does the Bible Say?
2. Prayer: How Is God Leading Me in Prayer?
3. The Holy Spirit: What Is the Spirit Saying?
4. Conscience: What Does My Conscience Say?
5. Circumstances: What Do Circumstances Suggest?
6. Counsel: What Are My Counselors Telling Me?

7. Fasting: Should I Fast About This?

Chapter 3: Habits and Virtues

1. Prioritize Friendship and a Small Group
2. Nurture a Spirit of Humility
3. Practice a Lifestyle of Repentance
4. Commit to Personal Discipleship
5. Take Personal Responsibility
6. Create Personal Accountability
7. Practice Selfless Service

Chapter 4: The Full Armor of God

1. Truth
2. Righteousness
3. The Gospel of Peace
4. Shield of Faith
5. The Word of God
6. Prayer
7. "Satan, I rebuke you in the name of the Lord Jesus Christ."

Chapter 5: Habits and Virtues

1. Surrender to Jesus Christ
2. Engage in a Local Church
3. Cultivate an Attitude of Gratitude
4. Do Your Part by Faith
5. Regularly Renew Your Faith
6. Ask for Help

APPENDIX 2

How to Lead a Discussion Group

Whether you already have a group or want to start a new group, you can facilitate a lively, meaningful discussion about The Four Voices by following these guidelines:

1. Part of an existing group? If your group is an existing Bible study, fellowship group, prayer group, or adult education class, plan to meet for six or seven weeks and discuss the questions at the end of each chapter. Read on for additional suggestions.

2. Want to start a new group? Photocopy the Table of Contents and the questions at the end of a couple of chapters. Ask a few people if they would like to be in a discussion group that would read

the book and answer the discussion questions together at the end of each chapter.

This can be a group from work, church, your neighborhood, or a combination. The optimum group size is from six to twelve people, assuming some will have to miss a week occasionally. (If the group gels, you may want to suggest that your group continues to meet after you've finished studying *The Four Voices*.)

3. At your first meeting, get to know each other and distribute a copy of the book to each person. Ask each person to take 3 or 4 minutes to share where they are right now on their spiritual journey. Getting to know each other like this will make everyone feel more comfortable—and more likely to participate wholeheartedly in the discussions to come.

4. Strongly challenge everyone to read Chapter One ahead of your next meeting. Ask them to come prepared to answer the questions at the end of the chapter by telling them this story: A leader told me about a small group that was getting mixed results. He said, "The people who read the

book chapter before they come are growing, and those who don't read it are stagnant. The stagnant ones just can't understand why their lives are not changing." Like with anything else, they will get out of the group what they put in.

5. Suggested meeting format. Begin with an icebreaker question, such as, "Anyone have a particularly good or tough week?" For a one-hour meeting, a good schedule to follow would be the following:

- Discuss an icebreaker question (5 minutes).
- Discuss the questions at the end of the chapter (45 minutes).
- Pray as a group (10 minutes).

Always start and end on time—it builds trust.

6. Have coffee and other drinks available. If you meet over breakfast or lunch, allow an extra 20 minutes for eating.

7. Leading a discussion. You don't have to be an experienced Bible teacher to lead a discussion about The Four Voices. Your role is to facilitate a discussion, not teach the group.

The key to a successful discussion group is your ability to ensure that each member gets air-time. Your role is to encourage each person to share their thoughts and ideas on the weekly chapter. Never talk more than 25% of the time. If there's silence, don't try to fill the space. If someone asks you a question beyond your scope, simply say so and move on.

If a group member asks an off-the-subject question, simply suggest that you discuss that issue at a separate time. If someone dominates the discussion, privately ask them to help you draw out the more hesitant members of the group. Take each question in order, and make sure everyone has the opportunity to share.

8. For best results, call your group members each week. This can be a short call that simply expresses, "I'm glad you're in the group and I'll see you Thursday," for example. Calling each person helps them feel like a valued member of the group and encourages them to prioritize the next weekly meeting.

Send me an email at patrickmorley@maninthemirror.org if you have any questions!

End Notes

[1] Gill, Brendan, Late Bloomers, (New York: Workman Publishing Company, Inc, 1996), p. 40.

[2] Pascal, Blaise, Pensées, (London: Penguin Books, 1966, Thought #148), p. 74.

[3] Quoted by his widow, Edith, in a seminar attended by the author.

[4] https://www.pewresearch.org/fact-tank/2019/11/06/key-findings-on-marriage-and-cohabitation-in-the-u-s/

[5] Reinhold Niebuhr, public domain, see https://en.wikipedia.org/wiki/Serenity_Prayer/

[6] Pascal, Blaise, Pensées, (London: Penguin Books, 1966, Thought #131), p. 66.

[7] Hughes, Philip Edgcumbe, A Commentary on the Epistle to the Hebrews, (Grand Rapids: Wm. B. Eerdmans Publishing Co., 1977), p. 149.

[8] http://www.churchill-society-london.org.uk/RusnEnig.html

[9] "Short" should be understood in the context that "Bible time" is elastic: "With the Lord a day is like a thousand years, and a thousand years are like a day" (2 Peter 3:8).

[10] Sidebar: The thief who comes to steal, kill, and destroy in John 10:10 does not refer to the devil.

[11] As previously written, the natural person is "not able to not sin" but believers are "able to sin or to not sin."

[12] Myers, Kenneth A., All God's Children and Blue Suede Shoes, (Wheaton: Crossway Books, 1989), pps. xiv-xv.

[13] As a sidebar, notice how all three persons of the Trinity are connected together in this one verse.

[14] Hudson Taylor, public domain, see https://theranch.org/2004/10/26/james-hudson-taylor-many-christians-estimate-difficulties/

[15] https://www.cru.org/us/en/train-and-grow/spiritual-growth/the-spirit-filled-life.html

WOULD YOU OR
SOMEONE YOU
KNOW CONSIDER A
CAREER IN **MEN'S
DISCIPLESHIP?**

**MAN IN THE MIRROR IS NOW RECRUITING
MEN IN YOUR COMMUNITY WHO ARE:**

 passionate about following Christ

 called to build God's Kingdom in
and through the church

 willing to put in a hard day's work
knowing that men are being saved
for eternity

BECOME A CHANGE AGENT

For more than 30 years, Man in the Mirror has been devoted to helping rescue men and their loved ones through the **transforming power of Christ.**

Behind every story of changed lives are our Change Agents, a special community of partners who give at least **$1 a day** to the mission of reaching men. Through the partnership of people like you, men's discipleship is impacting marriages, families, communities, and the world. **Discipleship changes everything.**

Be the change today.
**maninthemirror.org/give
or call us at 800.929.2536**